THE COLLAPSE OF THE BRITISH LIBERAL PARTY

Fate or Self-Destruction?

PROBLEMS IN EUROPEAN CIVILIZATION

THE COLLAPSE OF THE BRITISH LIBERAL PARTY
Fate or Self-Destruction?

EDITED WITH AN INTRODUCTION BY
J. A. Thompson
UNIVERSITY OF KENTUCKY

D. C. HEATH AND COMPANY
A Division of Raytheon Education Company
Lexington, Massachusetts

Table of Contents

v

II. DISINTEGRATION OF THE PARTY
    AFTER 1914?

Introduction

I n 1899 the *Nineteenth Century,* a leading Liberal monthly, published a symposium of articles on the "Liberal Collapse," in which four writers dilated on the waning fortunes of the Liberal party. The apprehension that prompted the series was understandable. For more than fifty years after the Reform Bill of 1832 a Liberal-Whig coalition had formed, with only a few interruptions, a regular government, and the Conservatives seemed destined to become a permanent opposition. After 1886, however, the pattern had threatened to reverse itself. Except for a brief term of office in the mid-1890's, the Liberals were not to hold office for twenty years.

The editors little expected their title to prove prophetic, however, and the "collapse" to become permanent. But 19 years later, in the election of 1918, the historic party was reduced to a mere shadow of its former greatness: only 26 members sitting in the House of Commons as a third party. The Liberals continued to poll millions of votes and the party to exist in shrunken form, but the harsh verdict of the electorate was never reversed, and the Liberals disappeared as a major political force.

Because the collapse was not absolute, the emerging Labour party was unable to claim the full heritage of power on the political left, and this fragmentation confirmed the Conservatives in power. They generally possessed crushing majorities from 1918 to 1945, and again from 1951 to 1964. Labour assumed the Conservative role of 1832-1886 and the Liberal position of 1886-

1906: long in opposition and seldom in office. The Conservatives, with only an occasional displacement, remained fastened in power as the permanent government.

Much of the fascination in the Liberal collapse lies in this Conservative monopoly of power: As Trevor Wilson has commented:

. . . whether one views the downfall of the Liberal party as triumph, or tragedy, or neither, depends ultimately on whether one regards the past half-century of Conservative rule as a blessing, or a misfortune, or as a matter of complete indifference.

With the Liberal collapse came also a change in the nature of British politics. Parties became divided more narrowly along class lines, politics more ideological in content, and class conflict noticeably sharper. Before 1918 the two parties were, in the words of Harold Laski, "a single party in control of the state," although "divided, no doubt, into two wings." They were, according to Arthur Balfour, agreed on the "essentials of society."

Between the wars, however, the cleavage was fundamental. The Conservatives were committed to private ownership, and the Labour party to a socialist base outlined in the celebrated Clause Four of their 1918 constitution:

To secure for the producers by hand and brain the full fruits of their industry, and the most equitable distribution thereof that may be possible, upon the basis of the common ownership of the means of production and the best obtainable system of popular administration and control of each industry or service.

The symposium of 1899 also foreshadowed future interpretations on the permanent collapse. The views expressed in the *Nineteenth Century* were repeated, with one variation or another, by commentators after 1918. Two of the writers in 1899 examined the "troubled soul" of Liberalism in terms of personalities and party policies. Specified actions, if followed, would lead to recovery. On the other hand, Keir Hardie and Ramsay MacDonald, speaking for the Independent Labour Party, forecast a permanent collapse of the Liberals. The demise of the Liberals was in the "nature of things," and it was "socialism that would inspire the progressive forces of the twentieth century as Individualism inspired those of the nineteenth."

Another contention, which could not have been foreseen in 1899, also divided historians later. When, they asked, was the Liberal party clearly in a state of decline, making a permanent collapse likely or inevitable? Responses to the question fall on either side of a chronological landmark: 1914. One school of historians finds the party disintegrating before the war, and the conflict only accelerating the process. The opposing school maintains that the disintegration set in during the war, prompted by war-time pressures, or as the result of political blunders perpetrated between 1914 and 1918.

These disputes raise the primary questions posed in this book. Was the collapse of the Liberal party "in the nature of things"? Did irresistible forces of history dictate the downfall? Or, if a permanent collapse was avoidable, what was the formula of recovery? Which mistakes were made? Who made them? And lastly, when was the party disintegrating with all avenues of recovery fully closed?

The readings below cluster around these questions. They give us, in the process, a set of controversial judgments, and make the Liberal collapse a fascinating problem of historical interpretation. The readings also reveal the difficulties faced by the parliamentary party as it tried to grapple with the complex social and economic problems of the industrial age. This book, therefore, may shed some light on the efforts of British parties currently seeking to govern a new technological society effectively.

In examining political parties, historians of England are increasingly fascinated by the silent social changes which make political shifts possible and intelligible. In the first selection, offered as an introduction to the entire problem, G. Kitson Clark, a distinguished specialist in Victorian studies, suggests this relationship between social change and political institutions. He does not examine the collapse of the Liberal party, but he does identify a new "social pattern" in late Victorian England that would force political change, and might lead to a displacement of the Liberals.

The second reading offers the provocative schema of the Marxists. Keith Hutchison, an economist, agrees with Hardie and MacDonald that class relationships are the key to historical events. The Liberal reforms of 1884 and 1911, he says, eased the inevitable transfer of political power from one class to another. This transfer spelled the doom of the Liberals, for the emancipated working class began to transform the political system to correspond with its own economic interests. The workers refused to accept a party which was both "herald of [political] emancipation and nurse of capitalism," and the historic role of the Liberals ceased after 1911.

The reformers in the 1860's certainly did not anticipate an outcome prescribed by Hutchison. They assumed that a reform of the franchise would end class animosities, that it would, in the words of William Gladstone, throw them into the shadows of oblivion. Did they over-simplify the point? Do parties naturally become champions of class interest? Was a working class party, and even a party with a socialist program, inevitable after the political reforms?

The radicals in the Liberal party did believe that political reform was linked to radical social legislation. The old Liberalism with its atomic conception of society, freedom of contract, and economic *laissez-faire*, they claimed, must give way to a New Liberalism. A writer in the *Nineteenth Century* described the new program in 1883 as:

> . . . regarding the state, with Burke, as 'the nation in its collective and corporate character,' sees in it the one sovereign agent for all moral, material and social reforms, and recognizes a special duty to deal with questions affecting the food, health, housing, amusements, and culture of the working class.

This brand of Liberalism encountered stubborn resistance in the party, but it appeared to dominate after 1906. In that year Winston Churchill announced that the "fortunes and interests of Liberalism and Labour are inseparably interwoven; they rise from the same force."

The reader may ask how deeply this new radicalism penetrated the party? Could the party transform itself, slough off the old Liberalism, and embrace a program of radical social reform? Could it do so before becoming outflanked on the left by Labour? Could radical reform alone appease the new electorate?

Sir Ivor Jennings, a Cambridge University scholar, takes up several of these questions in the second volume of his *Party Politics*. Jennings believes that the clue to voting and political parties lies in the class structure, and he therefore reflects some of the thinking found in the selection by Hutchison. He is not as rigid, however, and never speaks in terms of inevitability. The future of the Liberals, he says, lay in a "working-class" policy: the radicals provided the only "lucrative channels" in a democratic age. He also claims that several opportunities existed for such a shift in party gravity: especially with Joseph Chamberlain in the 1880's, and with Lloyd George and Winston Churchill after 1906. But Jennings claims that the party remained too classbound at all levels, and

that the leaders were uncreative on social issues. With such Liberal inhibitions he is not surprised to find a working class party emerging, or that it threatened to displace the Liberals even before 1914.

The reader may ask, however, whether or not Jennings has given the Liberals sufficient credit. Did the party not adopt a working-class policy by 1906? Was the New Liberalism not a wide departure from the Gladstonian tradition? Was the working class making any demands which the Liberal leaders were unable to meet? And on what evidence does Jennings base his judgment that Labour was already destroying the Liberals by 1914?

The fourth selection focuses more narrowly on personalities. J. L. Garvin, the official biographer of Joseph Chamberlain, believes that the radicals were on the verge of capturing the Liberal party in 1885. Chamberlain, the leading radical spokesman, was openly spoken of as a successor of Gladstone. That opportunity was squandered, he maintains, when Gladstone rashly committed the Liberals to Home Rule and drove Chamberlain from the party. Not only Home Rule for Ireland was at stake in 1886, but also the New Liberalism, for Gladstone and Chamberlain, differing on "ideas, visions, and desires," symbolized the two contesting traditions within the party. With Chamberlain's departure the radical tradition was weakened and, in Chamberlain's words, Gladstone had crowned his life "by the destruction of the most devoted and loyal instrument by which a great Minister was ever served."

This thesis always appealed to the radicals, but it rests on a number of assumptions open to challenge. The schism in 1886 and the loss of the Birmingham radical may have delivered the country into Conservative hands for twenty years, but was the party fatally weakened as the thesis implies? The Liberals triumphed in 1906 and were still in office after the elections of 1910. How was this possible if the party was bankrupt on social thinking after 1886?

Even if Chamberlain had replaced Gladstone, can Garvin or the radicals assume that he would have satisfied the new voters? He offered a radical social program: "to lessen the evils which poverty brings in its train, to increase the rewards of Labour, to bring hope to the miserable." But this only extended the hope of radical reform, not the abolition of the existing system. Chamberlain was deeply hostile to any attack on the principles of a capitalist economy. Would this win support in an era of high unemployment and economic vicissitude?

Several historians, while agreeing that the Liberal fate was linked to the social issue, take sharp exception to the judgments expressed in the first selections. Trevor Wilson, an Australian historian, argues that the Liberals were still thriving on the eve of the First World War. They had troubles, he concedes, but at most these suggested a loss of office, not a permanent eclipse. After examining election returns, he rejects the claim that Labour was making an inexorable march to power. Jennings and Garvin are also implicitly dismissed when Wilson claims that the Liberals before the war were making the difficult adjustment to the democratic age.

Samuel H. Beer, a noted American political scientist, refutes the claim that either the supremacy of Labour or the acceptance of socialism was inevitable. The new Labour party, he says, was only interested in "the organizational interests of the unions, the conditions of employment of their members, and the immediate circumstances of the lives of their members and families— in short, 'the interests of labour.'" These concerns could still be satisfied "on the premises of Radicalism." They did not include a demand for changing the "individualist and capitalist character" of the economy. In suggesting radical reform before 1914, according to Beer, the initiative came chiefly from the Liberals. The party was, then, still very much in the running.

Both Wilson and Beer contend that the war itself introduced a new set of conditions, upsetting Liberal progress, and throwing the initiative to Labour. But before 1914 they claim the Liberals were not doomed to near-extinction. The reader must decide if Wilson and Beer have built the proper interpretation upon the facts they present. Was the party's condition before 1914 as healthy as they suggest? Would the Trade Unions have remained satisfied with a secondary role in the Liberal-Labour association? Could the Liberals have continued to satisfy with a program of Radical social legislation?

John F. Glaser, an American historian, has approached the Liberal problem through a study of another powerful interest group in 19th century politics: the dissenting members from the Church of England. He emphasizes the sustaining influence of the Nonconformists upon the Liberal party. After 1850 Nonconformists became more militantly effective, and virtually captured the party as a convenient political instrument. It became a "secular church," and as Joseph Chamberlain claimed, Nonconformists were its hewers of wood and carriers of water. Before the war, however, Nonconformity was clearly on the decline, and Glaser argues that the ebbing of the Nonconformist influence had a corresponding effect upon the party strength. "An essential part of this greatness and decline of Liberalism was the greatness and decline of English Nonconformity. . . ."

The facts in Glaser's argument may be acceptable; but do they support his thesis? Is there indisputable evidence that Nonconformity would never recover and again buoy up the Liberal party? Perhaps, too, it was the war which rendered the dissenting message irrelevant and doomed both forces in Britain? Has he taken too narrow a view by selecting only one interest group?

Another provocative interpretation, also embracing an irresistible force, is promoted by George Dangerfield, in his *The Strange Death of Liberal England, 1910-1914*. He also has found a self-contained schema, in which he detects a pattern of violence reflecting a spiritual upheaval, in the years before the war. The various elements in his pattern—Tories, Irish, workers and suffragettes—engaged in violent rebellions which consciously destroyed nineteenth century values, and carried off that "highly moral, that generous, that dyspeptic, that utterly indefinable organism known as the Liberal Party." Dangerfield has written a sprightly account of the personalities and events in the pre-war years. Does his schema, however, withstand an empirical test? Was there a pattern of violence, or, in the phrase of Trevor Wilson, only "an accidental convergence" of violent movements? Were the problems that these forces presented insoluble? Was the inability of the government to meet its challenges the fault of the party, of Liberal values, or only of flabby leadership?

The interpretations of Part II fall on the post-war side of the chronological divide. In the first reading, Trevor Wilson argues that the war itself led to the downfall of the Liberal party by undermining the chief elements of its support, and by making its basic ideas irrelevant in the post-war world. As a secondary factor to the collapse, he offers the party schism of 1916. While the war menaced the Liberals, and the leadership struggle weakened its resistance, he contends that the conflict strengthened opposing political groups. The rise of national fervor, and the desire for military security, redounded to the favor of the Conservatives. The collectivist measures forced by the war experience, meanwhile, reinforced the Labour party on the left. The Liberals found themselves caught between two grindstones.

In the second selection, Samuel H. Beer approaches the Liberal collapse from the standpoint of the Labour movement. The war, he says, increased the "power, status, and even material condition" of the Trade Unions. This growth "virtually forced" Labour to break with the Liberals, and its independent bid for supremacy cast the Liberals into the shadows. The socialist program of Labour in 1918, he argues, was "functional to this choice of political inde-

pendence." To distinguish itself from other parties, Labour needed to pursue a new set of beliefs and values. It found them by embracing socialism for the first time.

The reader must decide if Wilson and Beer have successfully explained the party collapse and thereby refuted the judgments offered in Part I. Have they, in particular, given sufficient attention to the argument that the party was sadly weakened by struggles before 1914, and in that state was unable to resist the challenges after 1914?

Other historians, looking for self-destructive causes for the Liberal downfall, have focused upon Wilson's secondary theme. They maintain that the bitter leadership struggle of 1916 was the most serious—and destructive—ever experienced by the party. Roy Jenkins, a prominent Labour politician and biographer of Herbert Asquith, believes that the process of Liberal self-destruction began in 1916 with the displacement of Asquith, was confirmed by the Maurice debate of May, 1918, and was fully realized by the decision of Lloyd George to issue election "coupons" to a select number of Liberals later that year. In his examination of party struggles between 1916 and 1918, he holds Lloyd George primarily responsible for the shattering and final collapse of the party.

On the other hand, A. J. P. Taylor, a leading English historian, reaches a sharply divergent conclusion. A harsh critic of Asquith, Taylor emphasizes the demands of war, and the shortcomings of Asquith as the causes of Lloyd George's success in 1916. Asquith proved his incompetence before the struggle, says Taylor, and he ruined the party by his selfish refusal to serve under his former colleague. Appearing as selfish men, Asquith and his supporters received a *coup de grâce* at the hands of the electorate [not Lloyd George] in 1918.

In this dispute the reader must examine the evidence carefully and decide if the truth does not lie somewhere between the conflicting claims. One may also ask if the two men were not fighting over a spent party in 1916. Wilson claims that the party was decaying after 1914. Beer suggests that Trade Union strength made the rise of Labour inevitable. The historians in Part I claim that the party was destined to disappear anyway. Was the contest in 1916 one of the final stages in the decline, or the beginning of the collapse of the historic party?

These diverse interpretations are offered in the belief that there is value in searching for the "whys" and "hows" in history. They assume that such conflicting viewpoints must be encountered on the road to historical truth. The readings may also raise fundamental questions about history itself. Are there certain irresistible forces at work which overpower historical personalities? Do historical problems fit into self-contained schema, or do these only stand in the way of historical understanding? Is any role in the historical process left for personalities? The historian Albert J. Guérard has maintained that history is a matter of raising the right questions. This book has attempted to present a number of important questions about the collapse of the Liberal party. A study of the interpretations may lead to satisfactory answers.

The Conflict of Opinion

What probably in the long run determines the shape of politics are the social movements, the groupings and regroupings in the mass of the community, which are beyond the reach of politicians. . . .

———G. Kitson Clark

The immediate results of the Third Reform Act had been anticipated by neither friends nor foes. So far from proving the beneficiary of the enlarged franchise, the old Liberal Party was the chief victim . . . . In carrying the constitutional reforms from which it sprang to their logical conclusion—a democratic franchise—it sealed its own doom.

———Keith Hutchison

The future of the Liberal party after 1886 lay in an increasingly working-class policy. It was, however, ill-adapted to the change. Gladstone's predominance lasted until 1894, and he was too old to change his spots. Rosebery was in all essentials Conservative; and his line was followed by Grey and by the careerist young men from the middle classes, Asquith, Haldane and Morley. Harcourt was a lone crusader, and Campbell-Bannerman too weak and too ill to do more than keep the party together on the basis of Gladstonian policy, Home Rule and Free Trade. Lloyd George and Winston Churchill might possibly have diverted the Liberal party into more lucrative channels; but instead they had to fight a war. Already in 1914 the Labour party was beginning to destroy the Liberal party.

———Sir Ivor Jennings

The real danger to the Liberals was that in seeking to retain their "whigs" they might lose contact with Labour. Yet in 1914 this was not happening. The social reforming wing of the Liberal government was making the running. "Advanced" thinkers were still looking to Liberalism to implement their ideas. And Labour had put forward no major policy items which the Liberal party was unable to implement.

———Trevor Wilson

. . . even before 1914 the decline of Nonconformity had as an inevitable consequence the decline of Liberalism. The ebbing of the Nonconformist conscience entailed the gradual loss of the Liberal party's practical strength.

———John F. Glaser

Yet, before the curtain was hastily called down in August, 1914, Mr. Asquith and the Liberal Party of which he was such a placid leader had already been dealt a mortal wound. . . . the death of Liberal England—the various death of security and respectability—may not be considered simply as a loud prelude, passing suddenly into war. It was a brief but complete phase in the spiritual life of the nation.

———GEORGE DANGERFIELD

The outbreak of the First World War initiated a process of disintegration in the Liberal party which by 1918 had reduced it to ruins. As Liberals were often the first to recognize, the onset of war jeopardised the existence of a party whose guiding principles were international conciliation, personal liberty, and social reform.

———TREVOR WILSON

. . . it is hard to see how the powerful trade union movement, having reached the heights of power that it occupied in 1918, could have failed to break definitely with the Liberals and make its separate bid for political supremacy.

———SAMUEL H. BEER

Asquith mustered a vote [on the Maurice debate] of 108 . . . made up of 100 Liberals and a minority of the Labour members. The Government had 295, including 71 Liberals. Asquith and his followers went gloomily home. They could not have been pleased with themselves. They had been badly outmaneuvred. But they had no idea that they had participated in one of the great divisive debates of history, in an event from which Lloyd George would never allow the Liberal Party to recover.

———ROY JENKINS

Asquith . . . split the Liberal party and riveted on his adherents, however unwillingly, the appearance of opposing a government that was fighting the war . . . The "Maurice debate," though irrelevant to the war, was of historic importance. The official Opposition had divided the house against the government for the only time in the war. The Liberal party was split in two, a split that was never healed. On 9 May 1918 the historic Liberal party committed suicide.

———A. J. P. TAYLOR

INTRODUCTORY READING

Social Change and Political Parties

G. KITSON CLARK

As Reader in Constitutional History and Fellow of Trinity College at Cambridge University, G. Kitson Clark has advised his students to study the social changes behind the development of political parties. The essay below, based on the Ford Lectures delivered at Oxford in 1960, will suggest the value of such studies. Clark identifies the new social group late in the nineteenth century which would alter the structure and policy of the Liberal party.

A NEW SHAPE was forming in society. In the depressed and divided mass that had formed so much of the lower half of the section of the social life of England there was forming an organized and coherent body of workers, relatively prosperous, helping to form a body which was already an obviously important element in the State. In 1868 to advertise the position of this group the first Trade Union Congress was called together by the Manchester and Salford Council. Between 1867 and 1869 the whole position of the Trade Unions in the State was in fact reviewed with the assistance of Trade Union officials, and in the 'seventies, after a certain hesitation, the Trade Unions appeared to have achieved what they wanted in the definition of their legal position, though in fact a dangerous pitfall had been, through inadvertence, allowed to remain, which was going to cause trouble later on.

Of course, if this was the politics of class conflict it was indeed something very different from the emotional desperate half-revolutionary agitation of the 'forties: so much the progress of Victorian England had ensured. Indeed, it is difficult to see it as the politics of the class struggle at all. The Trade Union leaders at this time were often sober, practical men, in no way attracted by Utopian dreams; in politics they were normally Liberal or possibly in Lancashire Conservative, and would not have had any desire for a separate working-class party. It was their primary object to serve the interests of their members and to do so as far as possible without having recourse to strikes, which wasted the funds of their unions. Yet to understand what was moving in Britain it is necessary to recognize all this for what it was. It is the proper object of a Trade Union in any class of society to sell the services of its members at as high a value as it can, and it is the object of those who use those services to obtain them as cheaply as possible. The point was put with admirable simplicity by William Allan of the Amalgamated Society of Engineers to the Royal Commission on Trade Unions in 1867. "It is in their interest," he said of the employers, "to get the labour done at as low a rate as possible and it is ours to get as high rate of wages as possible." And that after all is the quintessence of the class struggle however soberly, practically and even amicably it is being carried on.

In fact, the class struggle was to have increasing importance in the next fifty years. The immediate future was, indeed, to be frustrating. In about 1873 the prosperity of Britain partially broke and with it the prosperity of the Trade Unions. In the late 'seventies and early 'eighties the movement was at a stay or in retrogression. But when it started again the situation had changed; not only the semi-skilled but the unskilled workers had come into the picture; there was more militancy, more conscious socialism, and men were moving towards the foundations of an independent labour party.

The Labour party is, however, beyond my field of vision. Indeed, from the vantage point of 1875, or even of 1880, it would not have been possible to say with assurance that an independent Labour party would develop in the form that it did, much less that it would displace the Liberal party. Even if an increasing insistence on the politics of the class struggle was likely there could be no certainty that events would take the particular course that they did take, especially under the impact of the peculiar circumstances of the years 1914–18. And in the years between 1860 and 1880 the current of events seems to favour the dynamic development of popular Radicalism. The most formidable political fact at that moment was the progressive development of the national Liberal Federation with its headquarters at Birmingham and its natural leader Joseph Chamberlain. This was, indeed, the full flowering of popular Radicalism; at this time advanced Liberalism was prepared to accept the lead of manufacturers such as Chamberlain and Mundella and yet to be able to gain the alliance of important sections of the working class, for the first Trade Unionist members of Parliament

entered the House of Commons under Liberal auspices. Capitalist, shopkeeper and workng man could still unite in the same cause. There was to be a greater emphasis on social reform than there had been in the past, but the cause was fundamentally the same as that for which Radicals had struggled in the 'forties, certainly the enemy was the same, the "titled and proprietary" classes against whom Bright had been fighting for twenty years.

Now, however, the battle promised greater hopes of success, and probably at least part of the reason for this was the greater diffusion of wealth through the country. The prosperity of the 'fifties and 'sixties had not only benefited sections of the working class, but to a much greater extent had enriched the various middle classes above them; the clerks, the shopkeepers, the business men and the directing and employing classes, all these had prospered and multiplied. The result was to facilitate changes which men had desired before 1850 but had not obtained. Before 1850 there had been the politics of distress and uncertainty, the difficulties of the late 'thirties and early 'forties had made many men very angry with the position claimed by the old governing classes; but their anger had effected little and then, after 1850, prosperity had developed to dull its edge and dissipate the attack. Now, however, the prosperity had worked its own changes, the numbers and wealth of those who were securely inside the old establishment had increased but the wealth and numbers who were not sure of their place in it had increased still more. Consequently it became difficult for the old privileged classes to retain their old position. The habits by which they had controlled the constituencies became increasingly inoperative, the leading positions which they claimed as their right began to be increasingly challenged, and new men or at least men using with new effect the appeal to the people began to emerge on the Liberal side of politics. In fact, the growth of the country under the continual influence of the blind forces of the increase of population and the Industrial Revolution had in the end created a country which could not be ruled in the old way.

* * *

It is convenient to take the year 1867 as the point at which the old régime began to break. It is, of course, to a large extent only a date of convenience. Much that took effect in the next twenty years had started before 1867. The increase and more general distribution of the wealth of the country had begun much earlier in the century. The relatively wealthy men who came forward to claim their place in the new constituency organizations had no doubt been developing their fortunes and their aspirations for some years before 1867, and the economic and social developments that seem to have given a new self-confidence and independence to many of the rank and file must have been maturing for some time. The nonconformist activities which were so important in the election of 1868 must be referred back at least to the activities of men like Miall and Richard[1] in the early 'sixties; in fact, the way was possibly prepared for them by the revivals of the 'fifties, certainly they were rendered effective by the growth in the number of nonconformists that had been going on throughout the century.

Nor . . . was the Act of 1867 an effective instrument of change. There was too little redistribution of seats to allow the newly enfranchised majorities their full power in the House of Commons. The qualifications for the franchise had now become so complicated and the problems they raised so difficult, particularly in relation to the lodger franchise and the vexed problem of compounding for rates, that it is difficult even now to know how many new voters

were enfranchised in particular constituencies. In several boroughs it was probably much less than we expected, while the country was still sealed off from the town with a higher voting qualification.

Nevertheless, on two important points the Act of 1867 signified a change. First it was the practical settlement of an important controversy. If the Reform Act of 1832 with all its defects had meant the final acceptance of the principle of progressive reform to meet the changing demands of the community, probably the Act of 1867 signified the acceptance, no less final, of the principle of democracy. Non-democratic elements still remained, and rejoiced in their strength. Those who did not accept the principles of democracy continued to find the prospect very disagreeable. The Liberal realists remained. The most trenchant expression of their views was probably James Fitzjames Stephen *Liberty Equality and Fraternity,* which was published in 1873, and the tendency towards Liberal realism seems to have inspired many of the Liberal Unionists in 1886. Nevertheless, in 1867 the dice were thrown. Those who feared democracy had said their say and had not been able to halt the course of events, and their could be no return or divergence, only a choice between delay and advance in one particular direction. The principle of democracy had been adopted, with whatever limitations it was going to be applied and whatever it might really mean in the actual disposition of power.

The other result of the Reform Bill of 1867 was more practical and immediate. In a good many constituencies there had been a considerable addition to the electorate, and in many constituencies these additions had been drawn from classes which had not been enfranchised before, changes which not only seemed to make new political developments possible but also a new type of constituency organization necessary. Therefore during the preparations for the election of 1868 the Liberals began to develop expedients in a good

[1]Edward Miall and Henry Richard, dissenting ministers and Radical politicians who, beginning in the 1840's, produced a school of aggressive politicians among dissenters. Miall was first elected to Parliament in 1852 and Richard in 1868. [EDITOR'S NOTE.]

many constituencies which gave some part in the choice of candidate to the working-class voter.

When, however, the election was over, particularly after the Reform League had started to come to pieces, there seems to have been a probably unconscious and undesired tendency for these methods to be dropped and more oligarchical organizations to be developed. It was probably a natural tendency. In the circumstances of the time it was not probable that political leadership would remain in working-class hands, and in a voluntarily organized, voluntarily financed institution power is likely to come to those who supply most of the funds. If it is possible to gain the necessary resources by a very large number of small subscriptions, then power is likely to be widely diffused through the whole association, if on the other hand it is necessary to depend on a small number of large subscriptions, then power is likely to be more concentrated; and it is probably always more easy to collect fairly large sums from a few deeply committed rich men than a great number of small sums from a crowd of small men whose interest in politics may not be very great.

But even if working-class participation was going to be less than had been expected, there were to be other reasons for changes in the constituency organization of the Liberals after 1870. For one thing there was the intense dislike which the Dissenters felt for the education policy of the Liberal Government and for those Liberal members who had supported it, and there were also the aspirations of wealthy and important men whose fortunes were of relatively recent growth who wished to force their way further into the party's councils than the older local leaders quite desired, while the prevailing emphasis on democracy encouraged the belief that the control of the party ought to rest with the rank and file rather than with a self-appointed oligarchy at the top. These ideas and this situation were exploited by Joseph Chamberlain and the other orga-

nizers in the foundation and development of the National Liberal Federation. The plan was to encourage the foundation of local Liberal Associations on the Birmingham model. The ultimate power in such Associations appeared to lie in ward meetings which the poorest Liberal could attend after paying only a nominal subscription, and they seemed so well suited to the democratic need of the moment that they were rather quickly developed in a variety of towns. In 1877 Chamberlain summoned a conference of these associations to Birmingham to found a federation, which should bring the representative system more effectively to bear on Liberal policy, and to be addressed by Gladstone, the rejected leader of the people, who had retired from politics after 1874 and who now mysteriously reappeared at their head inspired by profound anger at the atrocities of the Turk and the wickedness of Lord Beaconsfield.

In actual fact there was something delusive in the claims of the National Liberal Federation. As has often been pointed out the Birmingham Liberal Association was not truly representative in its government, the power did not in fact rise from the ward meetings and direct the affairs of the executive, it descended from the executive and the ward meetings did much as they were told. When the Liberal Federation came into being it was in fact more successful in reducing the personal independence of members of Parliament than in putting into effect the wishes of the rank and file. In several great towns there was a change of control at this time, but it was often not so much the transference of power to the people as the replacement of one rich man by another who was not very different in economic background and social position from those he displaced; sometimes it was no more than a change of generation. Most of this, however, was probably unavoidable, it was probably inevitable that the Liberal party should be controlled by a minority and at that moment by a wealthy minority. The idea that the control of any political party can lie in the hands of the rank and file is probably a phantasy, the mass of ordinary people are probably too inchoate, too confused in mind and too intermittent in their interest to give any definite lead, and the idea of democratic initiative is often the cloak for the operations of a small minority, to whose views the majority normally gives assent. Of course, if a section of the party feels that it is kept at arm's length, or new potentially leading personalities are misunderstood or opposed, there will be trouble. This was indeed to happen, for in due course the Liberal Party was to pay heavily for its failure to give working men a larger part in the control of its constituency organizations, a failure which can be studied in the mismanagement of Keir Hardie at the beginning of his career. But at that moment the natural leaders of the Liberals were probably wealthy industrialists, men like Chamberlain, Mundella and Sir James Kitson, who were prepared to promote a Radical policy. It was appropriate that power should rest with them, and at the moment, whatever its hidden defects, the National Liberal Federation was justified by success, for it participated on a very large scale in the great Liberal victory at the general election of 1880.

That was indeed a spectacular victory. At that moment it might well have seemed that Disraeli's Reform Bill had given the Liberals a permanent lease of power. The Liberals had won a decisive victory in 1868. It is true that they had been badly defeated in 1874, but there had been special reasons for that which were no longer valid. In 1874 the Dissenters had been at issue with the party, by 1880 they had been integrated into it. In 1874 many of the counties were still under an obsolete domination, in 1880 this seemed to be breaking up. In 1880, with their great leader at their head and with in many towns a new constituency organization presenting so it seemed the most advanced features of democracy, they swept into power. In 1884 they triumphantly re-

formed the electorate a third time and destroyed those anomalous pocket boroughs on which so much of the power of their adversaries had rested, at the same time they enfranchised the working man in the counties to complete the good work. In 1885 they were rewarded with another great victory, and at that moment there might have seemed to be every excuse to prophesy that even if the Liberals did not retain power permanently at least the Tories would never regain it.

In fact, the future was to be surprisingly and significantly different. The reasons for this are important. The simplest of them is that, as so often, political success produced its own antidote. When the party was being realigned on a new axis after 1865 and while it was being fused into a single whole by the volcanic powers of Gladstone's personality, it was natural that certain indigestible and recalcitrant fragments should resist this process and slip over to the other side. The movement started in the 'sixties when Palmerstonians such as W. H. Smith began to go over to the Conservatives, it reached its culmination in 1886 when large numbers of Liberal Unionists seceded at the time of Gladstone's first attempt to grant Home Rule for Ireland. This secession was the more drastic because the deserters included not only large numbers of the Whig nobility, and of the academic Liberals at Oxford and Cambridge, but also Joseph Chamberlain himself.

Even more important than this, there were areas of the country in which Conservatism was naturally strong, not because it was imposed by any dictatorial political control but because it was favoured by the people. There were also areas where by the natural process of events it was going to become strong. Conservatism seems to have had considerable natural strength in parts of Lancashire, partly deriving from feelings which dated from the time when the Tories had supported and the Liberals opposed factory legislation, and partly no doubt based upon the strong Protestant feelings which flourished wherever there had been a numerous invasion of the Roman Catholic Irish. This Lancashire Conservatism had its roots in past history; elsewhere Conservatism was being brought into existence by social changes in the country which had only recently become pronounced, in fact the same changes which in this period were altering the structure of the Liberal party. The basic cause was the greater diffusion of wealth. This had created a relatively prosperous and stable section of the working classes which at the moment, except in Lancashire, probably normally voted Liberal. It had improved the position of large sections of the lower middle class, who, at least if they were Dissenters, almost universally voted Liberal. No doubt such people were anxious for at least the appearance of greater political importance in party control than they had had in the past, and a policy which more nearly suited their susceptibilities than that of the Government which came into existence in 1868. The same process had also produced rich men who were anxious to play a leading role in the party and were attracted by a radical attack on the landed nobility. But this same diffusion of wealth had also inevitably produced a number of people who had reached an economic and social position which a radical policy on the part of the Liberal party might seriously threaten, or at best would not improve.

The extent of this social tendency has yet to be fully explored. It is not yet clear how far down the social pyramid it penetrated. Certainly in the upper ranges there had developed a group who had managed to develop to a greater or less extent what might be called the apparatus of a gentleman such as additional servants, a trap or carriage, special education for their children. In a good many cases the margin seems not to have been great, while the expense of maintenance increased continuously. They had therefore reason to fear the pressure of other classes; moreover they had become separated from the sympathies and class loyalties which their parents had entertained, and, as the third quarter of the century went forward, to an increasing extent they came to live in places remote from other classes and from the surroundings in which their parents had grown up. For as the cities grew and public transport improved, more and more of those who could afford it went to live in suburbs increasingly far from the centre of the town and the large masses of the working-class population.

This migration had very important social consequences. As has been said, in 1873 the Methodists drew attention to the serious implications of this tendency. They complained that it caused Wesleyans to desert the old chapels in the centres of the cities which numbered poor people in their congregation and said they, "not a few, moreover, have been lost to us altogether by this modern custom." But if lost to the Wesleyans, it seems not impossible that these might have been found on Sundays in the Anglican churches which were springing up in the outer suburbs, and if so the change might symbolize their adoption of the habits and feelings of the new single class communities which were coming into existence on the edge of the great towns, and which might well present to the Conservatives constituencies where their chances of success were very good indeed.

Amid the disappointments and disasters of the general election of 1868 there were here and there signs that these possibilities did exist for the Conservatives. There were successes in Lancashire, whither Gladstone had gone unmuzzled in 1865 and whence he now retired. W. H. Smith beat John Stuart Mill in Westminster and possibly, most significant of all, Lord George Hamilton defeated Labouchere[2] in Middlesex, a district which, as apparently the party managers did not yet realize, had recently become suburban. . . .

The Conservative party went forward

[2] Henry Labouchere, a prominent Radical and Member of Parliament, 1865–1906. [EDITOR'S NOTE.]

conquering and to conquer. 1886 seems to be one of the decisive turning-points in political history. Between 1868 and 1885 the Conservative party and the forces it represented in the country appear to be in irremediable decline while the Liberal party is in the ascendant. After 1886 the Conservatives enjoyed power till 1905, with the exception of the years 1892-95. In 1906 the Conservatives suffered a very severe electoral defeat, it is true, but they virtually returned to power in 1918 and have continued to hold it ever since with three short intervals, 1923-24, 1929-31 and 1945-51. No doubt these results can be interpreted in different ways, but however interpreted the contrast with the period before 1886 is remarkable, and it is heightened by the fact that the great Liberal party went into decline after 1918, a decline ironically much assisted by the working of the system of single member constituencies introduced by the Reform Act of 1884.

Of course, adventitious factors had much to do with this revolution of fortune. For instance, the ruin of the Liberal party was much assisted by the daemonic power of two Liberal statesmen of genius. The way that Gladstone handled the Home Rule issue between 1885 and 1886, and the way in which he handled Joseph Chamberlain probably made the rent at that date worse than it need have been; and the energy with which Lloyd George tore the party in two between 1916 and 1918 no doubt contributed a deadly blow at a moment of great political peril. But it seems probable that the misadventures of political history cancel out one against the other; there were certainly mismanagements and misfortunes on the Conservative side, and a terrifying electoral disaster in 1906, but their results were not so fatal. It also seems unlikely that one issue, like the issue of Irish Home Rule, really controlled the course of political history for more than a relatively brief period, in so far as it did control it over the whole electroral field at any time.

What probably in the long run determines the shape of politics are the social movements, the groupings and regroupings in the mass of the community, which are beyond the reach of politicians; and what happened at this moment has already been suggested. In the second and third quarter of the nineteenth century a mass of industrial and commercial wealth had come together at a central point in the social pyramid. It extended from the great manufacturers and merchants downwards through the shopkeepers and clerks to the upper ranges or the working class, the skilled workmen and craftsmen. The people in this section often differed widely in their ideas, their religion, their way of life and their politics. But enough of them resembled each other closely enough to supply the foundations of the great Liberal party which was the most important political fact in the country between 1865 and 1885. However, as is normally the case with the situations which such forces produce, at the very moment when one social pattern had become marked a close inspection could have shewn that the currents of change were preparing a new social pattern that would succeed it, and that in its turn would at least partially define the politics of the country for the next twenty years and probably for longer.

Speaking in very general terms, two processes seem to have been at work. At one point the increase in wealth, the increase in self-consciousness and confidence in a section of the working class had gradually created a new social group whose centre of gravity so to speak was at a lower point in the economic and social pyramid than in the group on which the Liberals had depended. More people in this group would have more markedly different interests from those who were the natural leaders of the old group than had been the case in the past, and they would want different things. Whether in fact this must necessarily have led to the replacement of the Liberal party by a Labour party it would be impossible to say, but it seems likely that if it had not done so an effective Liberal party in the second quarter of the twentieth century would have been very different in structure and in policy from the one which Gladstone led, or Chamberlain aspired to lead.

I. DISINTEGRATION OF THE PARTY BEFORE 1914?

Democratic Franchise Doomed Liberals

KEITH HUTCHISON

In 1950 Keith Hutchison, the financial editor of *The Nation,* published a study of British capitalism in order to show that the election of a Labour government in 1945 was not a sudden shift in British politics. The rise of collectivism was viewed as the inevitable outcome of economic and political forces set in motion by the extension of franchise in 1867 and 1884. He concludes that the Liberal party clung to power until World War I by skillfully making concessions to the working class, but its collapse, and the eventual rise of socialism, were dictated by "the forces of history." The elements of this Marxian thesis are lucidly expounded in the following reading.

Marx saw no possibility of compromise between capital and labor, and was certain that the inevitable triumph of the workers would come only after a violent upheaval, although he once admitted that in Britain the issue might possibly be settled without revolution. He never anticipated, however, what has actually happened—a Fabian retreat of the British capitalist forces before the slowly advancing political and industrial armies of labor. The most ironic of the contradictions of capitalism was, in fact, overlooked by Marx, although the evidence lay beneath his nose during his long years of exile in London. It was the peaceful surrender by the British bourgeois of their political monopoly, the preliminary stages of which had occurred before the socialist prophet died in 1883.

The paradoxical mission of nineteenth-century liberalism was to create both the free-market economy and the democracy that was to destroy it. To gain the first objective, the political monopoly of the aristocracy had to be smashed, but, having accomplished this end in 1832, the liberal bourgeoisie could not stop. For, while they might defend as a temporary expedient a franchise based on property, philosophically they were committed to equality of civic rights. Thus, hesitatingly and somewhat fearfully, they advanced step by step toward manhood suffrage, and so to the transfer of ultimate sovereignty to the masses. Henceforth the few who exerted economic power through the ownership of property became subject to the political authority of the propertyless multitude.

Beatrice Webb in *Our Partnership* summed up the inevitable conflict of interests that ensued:

The rule of the capitalist and the landlord has proved to be hopelessly inconsistent with political democracy. There can be no permanence

From Keith Hutchison, *The Decline and Fall of British Capitalism* (Hamden, Conn.: Archon Books, 1966 reprint) with foreword by David Owen and new preface by author, pp. xii-xiii, 25-26, 28-31, 101-113.

of social peace in a situation in which we abandon production to a tiny proportion of the population who own the means of production, and yet give the workers the political power to enforce demands on the national income which capitalism has neither the ability nor the incentive to supply.

The remarkable thing is that the British ruling classes were able for so long to retain a large, although gradually diminishing, measure of political and economic power. Their generals conducted the retreat with great skill, not infrequently delaying their adversaries by diversionary movements, sometimes winning useful periods of truce by modest concessions, occasionally staging temporarily effective counter-offensives. Nevertheless, over the years, they retired farther and farther from the spacious citadel which they occupied so confidently up to the last quarter of the nineteenth century.

*   *   *

The Radical Programme, a manifesto representing the views of Joseph Chamberlain, John Morley, and Sir Charles Dilke, issued in the spring of 1885, opened with the statement:

The Parliament of 1880 was elected by three millions of electors, of whom it was estimated one third were of the working-class. The next House of Commons will be elected by five millions of men, of whom three fifths belong to the laboring population.

This dramatic shift of ultimate political power was the fruit of the County Franchise Act of 1884, the third of the great reform measures that transformed Britain from an oligarchy to a popular democracy. It had ended the anomaly left by the Reform Act of 1867, which abolished property qualifications only for voters in the boroughs, by extending the suffrage to all householders in the county constituencies. The former arbitrary determination of voting rights by place of residence had excluded practically all the agricultural workers, a large number of miners who

lived in unincorporated towns and villages, and many industrial workers. A Glasgow boilermaker with a home inside city limits was a full citizen: if he moved across the Clyde to one of the suburbs in nominally rural Renfrew, he automatically became a political untouchable. Moreover, the restricted county vote had a much higher political value than that in the boroughs. The Redistribution Act of 1868 had left the rural areas greatly over-represented in Parliament. A voter in the sparsely inhabited Lake District, for instance, carried six times the weight of one in the populous, industrial Northeast.

Both the distribution of seats and exclusion of rural workers from the franchise had been designed, of course, to prevent the Tory Party, which was dominant in the countryside, from being swamped by rapidly expanding, normally Liberal, urban masses. Not surprisingly, therefore, efforts to persuade Parliament to take up the franchise question between 1874 and 1880, when the Tories were in office, proved futile. But after the great Liberal triumph of 1880, it was clear to Mr. Gladstone that reform could not long be delayed, although, according to his biographer, he himself was "not naturally any more ardent for change in political machinery than Burke or Canning had been."

The Liberal Prime Minister was in no great hurry, therefore, and it was not until the spring of 1884, at a time when his battered administration badly needed to repair its popularity, that the County Franchise Bill came before the Commons. "Never was there a bill," said Gladstone in his introductory speech, "so large in respect of the numbers to have votes; so innocent in point of principle."

*   *   *

The immediate results of the Third Reform Act . . . [were] anticipated by neither friends nor foes. So far from proving the beneficiary of the enlarged franchise, the old Liberal Party was the chief victim. Within its ranks, men who wished to woo the emancipated proletariat with more and more radical measures fought bitterly against those who stood pat on time-honored Whig principles. Torn by the conflict, the party found itself after the election of November 1885 without a working majority. The Liberals had won 82 more seats than the Tories, but the balance of power was held by a solid block of 86 Irish Nationalists. Gladstone had three choices: he could seek a coalition with the Tories; he could attempt to carry on without appeasing the Nationalists, which meant defeat the first time they chose to vote with the opposition; he could win Irish support by introducing a Home Rule bill. He decided on the third course and was shortly deserted by most of the Whigs and some of the radicals. This split put the Tories into office and kept them there for twenty years, except for a short interlude of weak Liberal government in the nineties.

In 1880 no one could have believed such a turn of events was possible. The election of that year had given the Liberals an over-all majority of more than fifty and left the Tories deeply despondent about their future. But the fact was that the Liberal Party, for all its seeming strength, had become an uneasy coalition of disparate forces. It had been built as an alliance between the Whig aristocracy, whose historic mission had been to reduce the power of the Crown, and the new business class. Both groups believed in a strict limitation of the sphere of the State. They had acquired from the classical economists, whose theories rationalized the needs of dynamic industrialism, a philosophy emphasizing a "natural" economic order to be achieved by releasing private enterprise from all restraints. Their political aim, therefore, was to remove every possible impediment to a free market in goods, labor, and money. This done, they believed, competition would remedy economic abuses and insure the "greatest good of the greatest number."

The Liberal Party had proved to be a great iconoclastic and purging force. It had swept away innumerable archaic nuisances;

abolished the rotten boroughs; cleaned up the eighteenth-century system of patronage and sinecures; reformed the Civil Service and the Army; ended religious tests and broken the educational monopoly of the established church; routed the mercantilist system with all its restrictions on trade and business; and much else. But in carrying the constitutional reforms from which it sprang to their logical conclusion—a democratic franchise—it sealed its own doom. The emancipated middle class had used its political power to create an economic system suited to its interests; there was every reason to suppose that, in the long run, an emancipated working class would insist on reshaping that system to conform with its own needs.

After the Reform Act of 1867, Liberal propaganda had to appeal to a growing number of working-class voters, and while at the Parliamentary level the party remained a Whig-business alliance, in the constituencies it was becoming a labor-middle-class combination. To labor, at least, the doctrines of *laissez-faire* were proving less and less satisfying. The enlarged scale of industry was diminishing opportunities for workers to rise from the ranks; the increasing number of businesses organized as limited liability companies was widening the gap between master and men. And unrestricted private enterprise, so far from proving a social panacea, was rapidly breeding new abuses and creating new problems. Willy-nilly, governments found themselves compelled to interfere with it in the interests of health and safety. Within the ranks of the Liberal Party there was a growing and vocal radical group with a social program it did not fear to call collectivist and a political program which included reform of the House of Lords and disestablishment of the Church of England. Such proposals were anathema to the still powerful Whigs, who had come to rest on their reforming laurels and were exhibiting increasingly conservative tendencies.

It was the political genius and personality of Gladstone that held the party together. In 1880, the "Grand Old Man" had passed his seventieth birthday but showed no sign of diminished powers. His long career had been molded by the pressures of his age and he had become the archetype of the emancipated bourgeois. He himself had sprung from that class as the son of a man who had emerged from a family of small traders to become a merchant prince of Liverpool, a proprietor of West Indian plantations, and the owner of numerous slaves. Sent to Eton, the young Gladstone had there been flogged by the famous John Keate, and so received the accolade that marks, and makes, the English gentleman. At Oxford he shone at Union debates as an exponent of deep-blue Toryism. One of his speeches opposing electoral reform made such an impression that shortly after receiving his degree he was offered Parliamentary patronage by the Duke of Newcastle and, at the age of twenty-three, entered the House of Commons. His first major speech was on a bill for the gradual abolition of slavery. It was a strong defense of the plantation interests coupled with a plea for the better religious education of their human property.

From such beginnings Gladstone had grown to become the unchallenged leader of the Liberal party, the champion of the oppressed in all lands, the keeper of the nonconformist conscience, the hero of the working classes, and the terror of his opponents. The most exalted of these last, Queen Victoria, was almost hysterical in 1880 at the thought of his replacing her beloved Dizzy. "The Queen," she wrote in her habitual third person, "will sooner *abdicate* than send for or have any *communication* with that *half-mad firebrand* who wd. soon ruin everything and be a dictator. Others but herself *may submit* to his democratic rule, but *not the Queen*."

Actually, Gladstone was anything but a revolutionary and was, indeed, quite out of sympathy with the socialist tendencies that were gathering momentum in the last years of his life. "I am thankful," he wrote to a friend after his final retirement, "to have

borne a great part in the emancipating labors of the last sixty years, but entirely uncertain how, had I now to begin my life, I could face the very different problems of the next sixty years. Of one thing I am, and always have been, convinced—it is not by the State that man can be regenerated and the terrible woes of this darkened world effectually dealt with." In the eighties he regarded himself, correctly, as a conservative influence. "Some of those you live with," he said to Henry Ponsonby in March 1881, "probably accuse me of being a radical. I am not. But I believe that I have the confidence far more than I deserve of those that are extreme radicals but who, as long as I am here, pay me that respect of following me in most of what I do. . . . But when I am gone younger men who will take my place will either be far more advanced than I have ever been, or will be forced on by the extreme liberalism of the masses."

Dread of "the extreme liberalism of the masses" was a dominant motif in the political thought of the time. Speaking in opposition to the County Franchise Bill, that timorous and class-conscious Whig, G. J. Goschen, had asked rhetorically: "Do we not see that democracy at every turn is clutching at the arm of the executive power?" Events were to prove that the emancipated masses, so far from greedily clutching at power, were for long to be content to pluck gently at its sleeve. Yet Goschen was right in stressing the revolutionary potential of an electorate with a large majority of workers who had no real stake in the existing economic system. If their votes were to decide who should govern, and on what principles, what hope had the upper classes of maintaining their grip on the State and so safeguarding the rights and privileges of property?

Walter Bagehot, in the introduction to his classic treatise, *The English Constitution*, had pointed out that the interests of "the aristocracy" and "the plutocracy" had become identical. Both were concerned "to prevent or mitigate the rule of uneducated members" and to succeed "they must not bid one against the other for the aid of their common opponent." Since the Tory Party broadly represented the aristocracy and the Liberal Party the plutocracy, a merger might have been logical. But political organizations, however similar their objectives, do not easily coalesce. Moreover, a naked alliance of the forces of property would be likely to provoke a united front of the workers. In politics, as in business, the strongest monopolies are those that maintain a convincing façade of competition.

*   *   *

In 1906, for the first time in history, the benches of the House of Commons were occupied by something like a cross-section of the population. Until then, members of both traditional parties had been recruited almost exclusively from the upper classes; typically they were sons of peers, well-to-do rentiers, leading lawyers, and top-rank businessmen. Now, among the 377 Liberals elected, a majority of 84 over all other parties combined, there was a considerable small-business element and numerous professional men—teachers, journalists, social workers, promoters of good causes. In addition, in the place of the former sprinkling of workingmen, there were 53 representatives of labor, 29 of them belonging to a distinct Labor Party, the rest either miners or "Liberal-Labor" trade union officials. By contrast, the 50 bankers and 53 railway directors who had sat in the previous Parliament were reduced to 16 and 21 respectively.

The rejuvenated Liberal Party was nearly as diverse in its points of view as in its social origins, and the ties binding it together were common antipathies rather than common sympathies. Generally speaking, members of the party were against tariffs, Chinese contract-labor, State support of religious education, and the drink interests. Their positive economic philosophies ran the gamut from Spencerian individualism to Fabian socialism. They formed anything but a tightly knit organization,

and the fact that it held together surprisingly well must be ascribed to the glue gratuitously supplied by Tory tacticians.

In constructing his government, Sir Henry Campbell-Bannerman had found places for representatives of all the main groups. He himself was a Liberal of the old school, a believer in Peace, Retrenchment, and Reform, but more sympathetic with the new democracy than Gladstone had been. A man of integrity and forthright speech, he had suffered unpopularity within his party and without when he had condemned as "methods of barbarism" the burning of farms and the use of concentration camps in the later phases of the South African war. The defeated Boers had not forgotten his courage, and the memory assisted his successful negotiation of the Union of South Africa—the outstanding achievement of his brief premiership.

The Cabinet included a number of other Gladstonian veterans, among them John Morley (India Office), Herbert Gladstone (Home Office), and Lord Loreburn (Lord Chancellor). But Campbell-Bannerman had been constrained to give key positions to his former opponents, the leaders of the Liberal Imperialists. H. H. Asquith became Chancellor of the Exchequer and heir apparent; Sir Edward Grey, Foreign Secretary; and R. B. Haldane, Secretary for War. The radicals were represented by David Lloyd George at the Board of Trade and a number of undersecretaries, including several friends and disciples of the Webbs, who were thus encouraged in their hopes of permeation. The most notable junior, however, was Winston Churchill, who, since parting from the Tories on the tariff issue, had been moving steadily to the left. His chief was in the House of Lords, so that as Under-Secretary for the Colonies he spoke for his department in the Commons during the important South African debates—an opportunity of which he made full use. Finally, John Burns was appointed President of the Local Government Board, the first workingman to hold Cabinet rank.

The election of 1906 was a shattering experience for the Tories. In 1900 they had returned 380 strong: now they were an attenuated band of 157. They had been swept out of most of the industrial districts —all nine of the Manchester and Salford seats, including Balfour's own, had been lost—and many of their rural strongholds had fallen. Only in Birmingham and Liverpool, the London suburbs, and the Home Counties, had they held their own. For the representatives of a class who regarded rule as their natural right, who believed sincerely that only members of their class were fit to govern, the situation was almost desperate. Everything they stood for appeared to be jeopardized by the mob returned to Westminster—a mob of dissenters, proletarian agitators, shopkeepers, and cranks. Right inside the Cabinet were such dangerous characters as the "red" John Burns and the foxy, pacifist, radical, Welsh solicitor—Lloyd George. This was democracy run riot, the nemesis Conservatives had feared in 1884 and then forgotten during two decades of power. Now the future of their country—which they instinctively identified with the fate of their order—seemed threatened.

Nevertheless, little save fear and a thirst for revenge united the Tories. The tariff[1] had been one of the main causes of their downfall, but ironically the wholehearted followers of Chamberlain had emerged as the strongest section of the party, comprising more than two-thirds of the elected members. Their leader seemed to be in a position to take over the whole party until in July 1906 he suffered a stroke which effectively ended his political life. Thus Balfour, for whom a safe seat was soon found, continued to command an unhappy Tory company in the Commons. In the Upper Chamber the vast Tory host was captained by the Marquess of Lansdowne, former Whig grandee and owner of large Irish properties, who shared Balfour's apathy on the tariff question.

Despite this disunity between leaders and led, a façade of party harmony was erected and tacit agreement reached on a strategy to hamstring the Liberal Government and nullify as far as possible the verdict of the electors. The chosen weapon was the veto power of the House of Lords which since 1886, when most of the Whig peers broke with the Liberal Party on Home Rule, had become for all intents and purposes a Tory club. Constitutionally, this change had put the Lords in an exposed position. It was difficult enough in any case to reconcile an unrepresentative, hereditary Upper Chamber with popular democracy: it was impossible to justify one controlled not only by a single class but by its most conservatve section. The claim made was that the House of Lords performed a useful function in revising hasty legislation and in checking governments that had exceeded or outlived their mandates. But in fact it operated as a brake only when Liberal hands were on the wheel; when the Tories were in office, it was little more than a rubber stamp.

Writing to Lansdowne on April 13, 1906, Balfour said:

I do not think the House of Lords will be able to escape the duty of making serious modifications in important government measures but, if this be done with caution and tact, I do not believe they will do themselves any harm. On the contrary, I think it quite possible that your House may come out of the ordeal strengthened rather than weakened by the inevitable difficulties of the next few years.

Seldom has so brilliant a mind made so poor a calculation. . . .

The Tory aim was to cut down the Government's legislative program without raising an issue on which the Liberals could appeal to the electorate in the hope of receiving a mandate to "end or mend" the House of Lords. Among the more notable victims of this policy of selective slaughter were the Education and Plural Voting

[1] Chamberlain left the Balfour cabinet in 1903 in order to lead a campaign for tariff reform. The issue split the Conservatives and helped unite the Liberals. [EDITOR'S NOTE.]

Bills of 1906 and the Licensing Bill of 1908, all measures offensive to Tory vested interests. The first sought to end denominational teaching in the public elementary schools and to excuse children of dissenters in rural districts, where often only Church schools were available, from attending religious instruction. This attempt to meet nonconformist demands was objectionable not only to the Church of England but also to the Roman Catholics, so that the Tories were able to enlist the support of the Irish Nationalists and Catholic trade unionists. It was not, therefore, a measure commanding such overwhelming support that the Government was likely to risk a dissolution. A more dangerous action, perhaps, was the Upper Chamber's unceremonious dispatch, with little more than a pretense of debate, of a bill to abolish plural voting. This system, which permitted electors to vote in each constituency in which they owned property, gave a privileged position to landowners and businessmen from which the Tories benefited much more than their opponents.

Infuriated at the defeat of this long-promised reform, the Commons retorted with a resolution, carried by 432 to 127, calling for limitation of the right of the Lords to amend or reject legislation. Unheeding, the Tory peers went on to kill the Licensing Bill, the main purpose of which was to reduce the total number of public houses. This step, favored by temperance reformers in all parties, was naturally anathema to the brewing interests; and not even a personal appeal to Lansdowne by the King moved the Tory peers who, meeting in conclave at Lansdowne House, decided by a huge majority to reject the bill. The subsequent discussion and vote in the House of Lords was, therefore, a mere formality.

Lloyd George's charge that the House of Lords "was not a watch-dog of the Constitution but Mr. Balfour's poodle" seemed to the Liberals more than ever justified. But they still needed an issue to fire the country, some "measure of social legisla-

tion whose effects would be so far-reaching that the House of Lords could neither accept it without humiliation, nor reject it without imperilling its prerogatives and even its existence." Left to himself, Asquith, who had become Prime Minister in 1908, might not have forced a showdown. He was an able advocate, a cool and resourceful Parliamentarian, and an amiable Cabinet chairman. He was not a fighter and most of the reforming zeal of his youth had evaporated. John Morley once said that he had "not only a constitutional disinclination to anticipate events, but a reasoned conviction that in nine cases out of ten a decision is best deferred till the last moment." John Dillon, Irish Nationalist M.P., complained to Blunt that Asquith, who had once been unpretentious, had now "adopted all the feelings of the aristocracy," and asserted "he had been ruined by his second marriage to one[2] who was a Tory at heart and was always advising him to stand out against Lloyd George and Churchill and the mass of the Radical Party."

The Prime Minister's lack of drive was more than compensated for by the aggressive energy of Lloyd George and Churchill who together devised a strategy to beat the Lords and took charge of its application. The little Welshman had proved an outstanding success at the Board of Trade and, when the ministry was reshuffled on the retirement of Campbell-Bannerman, had won promotion to the Treasury. Churchill's talents had also brought him rapid advancement. After a brief apprenticeship as Colonial Under-Secretary, he had followed Lloyd George at the Board of Trade and in 1910 was to become Home Secretary. In both these offices he played an important part in shaping and carrying through the social reform program, winning the approval, not lightly bestowed, of Beatrice Webb. His chief interest, he told Blunt in 1909, was the welfare of the poor. "I would

[2] Margot Tennant, a gifted writer and leader of society who married Asquith in 1894. [EDITOR'S NOTE.]

give my life," he said, "to see them placed on a right footing in regard to their lives and means of living. That is what I am paid for."

Plans for an ambush of the Tory peers, whom success had rendered complacent, seem to have been laid in September 1909 when Churchill visited Lloyd George in North Wales. Early in the new year, the former, in a speech at Birmingham, gave a hint of what was being plotted:

I do not, of course, ignore the fact that the House of Lords has the power, though not I think the constitutional right, to bring the government of the country to a standstill by rejecting the provisions which the Commons make for the financial services of the year. . . . And for my part, I should be quite content to see the battle joined as speedily as possible upon the plain, simple issue of aristocratic rule against representative government, between the reversion to protection and the maintenance of free trade, between a tax on bread and a tax on —well, never mind.

Not all Lloyd George's colleagues were as willing as Churchill to aid and abet his scheme for humbling the Tories and, incidentally, "dishing the Socialists," by a radical challenge to the House of Lords. Most members of the Cabinet belonged, or were closely allied, to the propertied classes, and it was not without misgivings that they approved "the People's Budget." However, they had no alternative to Lloyd George's plan for dealing with the Second Chamber's successful sabotage of the Government, and it was clear that commitments for expenditure made a large increase in taxation inevitable in 1909. Old-age pensions had proved more costly than anticipated, and other money-absorbing social reforms were in contemplation. A rapid increase in motor traffic necessitated a large road construction and modernization program. Last but far from least, naval building plans were being accelerated with the vociferous approval of most of the press, the armament industry, and the Tory Party. The budget was bound to be a big one: why not make it "popular" as well?

Altogether the Chancellor of the Exchequer had to find £16 million in new taxation—a larger addition than any of his predecessors in office had ever been required to raise in peacetime. Apart from social theory, or a desire to confound opponents, he was compelled to rely mainly on direct taxation. The trend of financial policy had been in that direction for years, and the Labor Party was pressing for heavier levies on large incomes and reduction of the consumption taxes that burdened the poor. In 1907, Asquith had taken a new step toward income-tax reform by setting a lower rate for earned incomes below £2000 and had increased death duties on estates exceeding £150,000. Lloyd George went considerably further toward a fully graduated system of direct taxation. Incomes over £3000 were to pay 1s 2d in the pound instead of 1s and those over £5000 became liable to a supertax of 6d in the pound on the amount by which they exceeded £3000—an idea borrowed from the, then, fiery socialist, Philip Snowden. Steeper graduation of death duties applied the maximum 15 per cent rate at the £1 million level instead of £3 million and, to check evasion, provision was made for the taxation of gifts.

"Soaking the rich" in this manner could not provide enough revenue, and Lloyd George was forced to turn to consumption taxes on drink and tobacco. That too served his reforming purposes, for he believed in "making as difficult as possible the access of the people to any commodity that injures them." Moreover, increases in duties on beer and spirits, together with a steep rise in the tax on liquor licenses, struck a blow at the Tory drink interests and afforded revenge for the defeat of the 1908 Licensing Bill.

The forces of property found all these tax increases unfair and burdensome, but what really aroused them to berserk fury was a series of entirely new taxes on land. These were four in number: (1) a 20 per cent levy on increases in site values accruing after April 30, 1909, payable when land changed hands; (2) a 10 per cent charge on the added value received by a lessor at the end of a lease; (3) an annual tax of one halfpenny in the pound on the value of undeveloped sites; (4) an annual tax of 5 per cent on mineral royalties. Only the last of these imposts was expected to produce any appreciable revenue immediately: from the others the yield, at best, would expand slowly after the laborious task of making a complete land survey and valuation—"a new Domesday Book"—had been concluded. The concern of landowners, however, was with ultimate consequences. It appeared to them that a precedent was being set and a technique developed which could lead to confiscation; that these "vindictive and socialistic" taxes were, in the words of Sir Edward Carson, "the beginning of the end of all rights of property."

In the perspective of history, their anguished rage appears quite disproportionate to the provocation. Lloyd George, like Joseph Chamberlain in the eighties, was seeking to attach the masses to the Liberal Party by posing as their champion against aristocratic privilege. But he was inviting them into that economic blind alley which commemorates Henry George rather than leading them along a broad highway to socialism. The fury of his opponents aided the deception. The more they sought to paint him as "a swooping robber-gull" (Lansdowne's phrase), the more successfully he dramatized himself as a modern Robin Hood who made the landlord and the capitalist pay for security of property with premiums which could be used to improve the conditions of the poor.

In the House of Commons the Tories could only conduct a fighting retreat: even with the help of the Irish, whose own quarrel with Lloyd George had been excited by the increased tax on whiskey, they could not hope to upset the Government majority. There remained, however, their majority in the Lords, a potential weapon against the budget, but one whose use raised grave constitutional questions. Since the seventeenth century, the House of Commons had claimed exclusive rights to determine national revenue and expenditure. This privilege was not formally enshrined in any statute but rested, like most constitutional practice, on a formidable set of precedents. The last occasion on which the Lords had tampered with taxation was in 1860, when they threw out a bill abolishing the paper duties, a move which the Liberal Government of the day claimed was amendment of the budget by indirection. The following session, therefore, it had incorporated in the Finance Bill all tax changes, including cancellation of the disputed duties, and the Lords, unwilling to take responsibility for rejecting the bill and forcing a general election, had capitulated. Salisbury, at the time of Harcourt's "Death Duties Budget, had spoken of noninterference of the Second Chamber with finance bills as "accepted practice"; Balfour, as recently as October 6, 1908, had said in a speech of Dumfries: "It is the House of Commons, not the House of Lords, which settles uncontrolled our financial system." Thus, as an astute writer has put it:

The question now was—how silly would their lordships be? By constitutional tradition, they could veto everything but a Budget: yet here was a Budget crying to be vetoed. It was like a kid, which sportsmen tie up to a tree in order to persuade a tiger to its death; and at its loud, rude bleating the House of Lords began to growl.

Some of the Tory elder statesmen saw clearly enough that the peers could not kill the budget without exposing themselves to a crippling blast of Liberal bullets, and urged caution. But whenever the tiger showed signs of retreat, Lloyd George found means of exciting it anew. In his famous Limehouse speech on July 30, 1909, he mixed taunts with pathos, contrasting the insolence of wealth with the "patience and fortitude" of the people. At Newcastle on October 9, a few weeks before the Upper Chamber began to debate the budget, he dared the peers to do their worst. The question was, he said:

Should 500 men, ordinary men, chosen accidentally from among the unemployed, override the judgment—the deliberate judgment —of millions of people who are engaged in the industry which makes the wealth of the country.

From his invalid's couch, Joseph Chamberlain, forgetting he had once proposed a "ransom from the rich," declared that the issue was between tariff reform and socialism and begged the House of Lords "to force an election." His deluded followers thought that an appeal to the country would probably give them both power and the long-sought mandate to introduce protection. Thus tariff reformers and the landed interests, the manufacturers and the aristocracy, were more than ready to accept the lead given by Lord Milner who declared on November 26 that the duty of the peers was "to try to prevent a thing they believed to be bad and damn the consequences."

Four days later, the House of Lords rejected the budget by 350 to 75 and the consequences became manifest. On the motion of the Prime Minister, the House of Commons solemnly agreed that the action of the House of Lords "is a breach of the Constitution and a usurpation of the rights of the Commons," and Parliament was then dissolved. There was no doubt about the major issue on which the election was to be fought. The budget had become of secondary importance, and the Liberal Party was asking the voters to give them authority to reduce the powers of the Upper House so that its Tory majority would no longer be in a position to veto legislation distasteful to it.

The results of the election of January 1910 were disappointing to both major contestants. Almost exactly equal numbers of Liberals and Tories were returned, and the former now had to depend for a majority on support from the 40 Labor members and the 82 Irish Nationalists. It was the Irish who really held the balance of power and the previous year they had voted against the budget. Now they were prepared to sacrifice their whiskey, but only on condition that the Government gave the most binding assurances that the wings of the House of Lords would be clipped so that it would no longer be in a position to veto Home Rule. On these lines an understanding was reached, thus making inevitable a battle over Ireland as soon as the supremacy of the Commons had been secured.

There is no need to retell in detail the oft-told story of the struggle over the Parliament Act, which finally received the Royal Assent in August 1911. The battle was interrupted for some months following the death of Edward VII in May 1910, when, to meet the wishes of his successor, George V, leaders of the two major parties explored the possibilities of compromise. No meeting of minds proved possible. The Tories were willing to reduce the hereditary element in the Upper Chamber, but only if its membership was reformed in such a manner as to insure a permanent Conservative majority, and if it retained at least sufficient power to force a general election on a constitutional or "organic" issue, such as Irish Home Rule. To the Liberals, on the other hand, reform of the composition of the House of Lords was a matter of minor interest; their purpose was to make it definitely subordinate to the Commons and responsive to the will of the electorate. It was easier to accomplish this end if the Upper Chamber continued as a palpably undemocratic body with "no damned nonsense of merit about it."

When the inter-party conferences failed, the Government proceeded with its plans to enact the Parliament Bill. This measure provided that: (a) the House of Lords should henceforth be without power to reject or amend any bill certified by the Speaker of the House of Commons to be a "Money Bill"; (b) other bills, when passed by the Commons in three successive sessions and rejected twice by the Lords, should become law, provided that there was an interval of two years between the second reading of the bill for the first time and the final third reading; (c) the maximum duration of Parliament should be reduced from seven to five years. Although drastic, the bill still left the House of Lords considerable scope for influencing legislation. Since the procedure prescribed for overcoming resistance in the Upper Chamber was so time-consuming, governments were likely to avoid resort to it by accepting amendments to legislation unless vital questions of principle were involved. Further, the two-year-interval provision meant that the Lords' veto would become effective after a government had been in office three years—a fact which assumed importance in 1948 when the Labor Government faced the prospect of legislative impotence during the two years that remained to it.

Thanks to the Parliament Act of 1911, Mr. Atlee's administration could seek a remedy by introducing a bill, restricting still further the Lords' suspensive veto, in time for its passage in three successive sessions before an election was due. In 1910, Asquith faced a much more difficult problem: before his bill could become law he was compelled to obtain the consent of the Upper Chamber to the amputation of its own powers. There was only one final sanction available—use of the Royal Prerogative to create peers in sufficient numbers to give the Government a majority. This threat had been successfully used to force through the Reform Act of 1832, but its employment was a matter of considerable delicacy if the Throne were not to become directly involved in party politics. It was not, therefore, until the end of 1910, when it was certain that the House of Lords was going to reject the Parliament Bill and force yet another general election, that the Cabinet asked the King to be ready to exercise his Prerogative if the voters again endorsed the Liberal policy and the Lords once more sought to override their decision. The King consented to furnish this club, but Asquith was not disposed to flourish it before the contingency

for which it was designed actually arose.

It was, perhaps, unfortunate that the Prime Minister kept his weapon so discreetly concealed. For to many noble lords it seemed incredible that the King would consent to allow their House to be swamped by 500 upstarts—a belief undoubtedly encouraged by some in Court circles who claimed to be "in the know." Such wishful thinking led them into reckless courses. "Let them make their peers," cried Lord Curzon in May 1911. "We will die in the last ditch before we give in." (Three months later he was to crawl out of that ditch, muddied by the abuse of tougher and more obtuse colleagues, to vote for the Parliament Bill and save the "order" in which he took such pride from ridiculous inflation.) Some of the more romantic Tories actually talked of revolution. In February 1910, George Wyndham, former Chief Secretary for Ireland, said to W. S. Blunt:

The strength of the Tory position is that they and the King together command the whole material force of the country, besides half its voting strength. They have the money, and the Army and the Navy and the Territorials, all down to the Boy Scouts. Whey then should they consent to a change in the constitution without fighting?

A year later he was harping on the same theme, urging that the Tory leaders should say to Asquith: "You threaten us with a revolution: we threaten you with a counter-revolution." Balfour and Lansdowne, the responsible heads of the party, knew better than to indulge in dreams of a twentieth-century Barons' Revolt. As a last gesture of protest they consented to sponsor a bill limiting the Prerogative of the Crown relating to the creation of peers—a curious proposal to come from a party which had originated as "the King's Men" and regarded itself as the peculiar buttress of the monarchy. But when, on July 20, 1911, Asquith sent letters to Balfour and Lansdowne declaring firmly that the King had consented to create sufficient peers to insure passage of the Parliament Bill, they knew the game was up. By this time, however, they had lost control of their followers. A group of peers, large enough to offset the maximum Liberal strength in the Upper Chamber, rallied to the banner of the octogenarian Lord Halsbury who refused to be intimidated by "this bogey of the Royal Prerogative." It was not sufficient, therefore, for the rest of the Tory peers to abstain; some of them had to sacrifice themselves, and Lord Curzon finally persuaded 37 to join the Liberals and most of the Bishops in the Government lobby. The bill was saved by 17 votes. "We were beaten," wrote George Wyndham, "by the Bishops and the Rats."

After the lapse of forty years, this whole episode has acquired the comic flavor of old-fashioned melodrama, and it is difficult not to laugh at the passionate rhetoric of the peers as they defended their home and honor against the villainous Liberal mortgageholders. Nevertheless, the fears that inspired their opposition were not so groundless as some historians have suggested. Undoubtedly, the Parliament Act weakened the political defenses of property and so assisted the subsequent advance of socialism. On the other hand, a victory for the House of Lords in 1911 might have proved even more dangerous for the inter-

ests it represented. It would have given notice to the masses that the Reform Acts had not secured popular sovereignty, that the will of a majority of the people could still be frustrated if it clashed with that of the upper class. It would have blocked the gradualist approach to social democracy and reinforced the Marxian thesis, hitherto neglected in Britain, that only revolution could bring emancipation to the working classes.

Thus in meeting and defeating the challenge of the House of Lords the Liberal Party once again cleared the constitutional channels to progress. And with this service it completed its historic mission. When the last serious political barrier to democracy was down, there was no longer scope for a party which had been both the herald of emancipation and the nurse of capitalism. Now that emancipation had acquired a socialist connotation, these two functions were openly in conflict and, as a consequence, the Liberal Party began to disintegrate, with some of its members pulled to the right and others to the left. Even if the First World War had not produced a fatal schism among the Liberals, it is doubtful whether they could long have remained a major force. The climate of the British Parliamentary system has never been kind to third parties.

Liberals Ill-Adapted for Change

IVOR JENNINGS

The Vice-Chancellor of Cambridge University, Ivor Jennings, has received much praise for his single-handed survey of the entire constitutional machinery of Britain: *Cabinet Government* (1936), *Parliament* (1938), and a three-volume study of *Party Politics* (1960-3). He belongs to the school of scholars who view political behavior as a reflection of class interests, but his treatment is sophisticated, balanced and analytical. Those characteristics are displayed in his consideration of the leaders of the Liberal party.

AFTER 1867 the urban electorate was predominantly working class. This did not mean, however, that the whole urban electorate either would or did vote for a dominantly working-class policy. The conflict of Liberal and Conservative was fundamentally not a conflict of working-class policy at all. It was a conflict between two sets of aristocratic and middle-class politicians over the matters which the wealthier classes thought important, like taxes on agricultural products, Home Rule, relations with France, the Russian menace, the Middle East, and what not. Class was relevant, but as emotion and prejudice rather than as a policy; and Disraeli was right in thinking that, other things being equal, many urban householders would rather vote for a landowner backed by a bevy of bishops than for a manufacturer of screws with a Nonconformist conscience. The political ideas of every man are conditioned by his upbringing and his environment; in the middle of the Victorian era it was proper to support one's betters. The boroughs, especially the great towns, were less subject to the tyranny of caste than the county constituencies; and generally the Liberals obtained more borough seats than the Conservatives; but it is far from true that the borough elector was

destined by his class to be a Liberal supporter. Joseph Chamberlain thought, and no doubt thought rightly, that the Liberals would gain by producing a policy which would appeal to the self-interest of working men; but he himself showed, by retaining his "pocket boroughs" after 1886, that Irish Union, imperialist adventures, and even Protection, could retain working-class support.

Nevertheless, it is plain that, in the long run, the conflict must be between traditional values, including respect for social superiors, together with a modicum of labour reform, on the one hand, and a positive working-class policy on the other. Given the two-party system already in existence in 1880, one would expect the Conservative party to support the one and the Liberal party to support the other. The dominance of Gladstone and the truculence of Joseph Chamberlain prevented this development in the eighties. The Conservative party was so strengthened that it inevitably became the supporter of traditional values (though, of course, the values kept changing with tradition) at least until 1918.

The future of the Liberal party after 1886 lay in an increasingly working-class policy. It was, however, ill-adapted to the

From Ivor Jennings, *Party Politics*. Volume II: *The Growth of Parties* (Cambridge, 1961). Reprinted by permission of the Cambridge University Press, pp. 284–285, 218–220, 250–251.

change. Gladstone's predominance lasted until 1894, and he was too old to change his spots. Rosebery was in all essentials Conservative; and his line was followed by Grey and by the careerist young men from the middle classes, Asquith, Haldane and Morley. Harcourt was a lone crusader, and Campbell-Bannerman too weak and too ill to do more than keep the party together on the basis of Gladstonian policy, Home Rule and Free Trade. Lloyd George and Winston Churchill might possibly have diverted the Liberal party into more lucrative channels; but instead they had to fight a war.

*   *   *

. . . generally the Liberal leaders were socially distinct from the Conservatives only because they were Liberals. They were even more separated by origin, education and association from the men of the lower middle class and working class who formed the main body of the Liberal electorate than the Conservative leaders are today from the great mass of the electrorate.

Campbell-Bannerman's Cabinet of 1906 was much like a modern Conservative Cabinet, though there was not such an emphasis on Eton and Oxford nor on inherited wealth. There were six peers and two baronets, seven Oxford men (four from Balliol) and five Cambridge men (four from Trinity College). The three Etonians were partly offset by two Harrovians, but Winchester, Cheltenham, Clifton and Wellington were also represented and nine of the nineteen members had not attended expensive public schools. Seven of the members had earned their way into politics, and there was even a working man, John Burns. Like the modern Conservative Cabinets, however, it was more aristocratic and upper middle class than the main body of the party supporting it, and for the same reason, that most Cabinet offices went to the "professional politicians" who were able to live on inherited wealth (or married it) and thus

to enter the House of Commons when young.

In any event, the richer members of the Liberal party usually had some knowledge of the problems of the back streets. The late Victorian and Edwardian period was the great era of "slumming," when great ladies put on their oldest costumes to pay visits to what General Booth had called "Darkest England." Only an unusual person, like Beatrice Potter (Mrs. Webb), would actually share the life of the East End, but Margot Asquith, for instance, before her marriage spent one lunch-time a week in a factory. The Majority Report of the Royal Commission on the Poor Laws (1905–9) proposed to hand over the administration of outdoor relief to organised charity, to rely on "the personal service and pecuniary assistance to be voluntarily afforded by the rich to the poor."

To the present generation the idea seems fantastic that under a system of what was virtually adult male suffrage the control of Government could be vested ultimately in two groups of rich men. Charles Booth had shown that thirty per cent of the population belonged to the "pauper class," the class in which employment was casual, intermittent or unstable. Above them was the main body of the working class, half the population; in steady employment but at the mercy of sickness or the trade cycle, with nothing between them and pauperism but the small savings in "the Co-op" or the Post Office Savings Bank. These were the "People with a capital P" whose votes Joseph Chamberlain had sought to catch by parts, at least, of the *Radical Programme*. They were the people whose votes the Radical wing of the Edwardian Liberal party, Lloyd George and Winston Churchill, sought to catch with old age pensions and social insurance. It is obvious to us now that if the rich wanted to govern in the Victorian manner they had to buy the privilege with heavy taxation and social services.

There are, however, reasons for the failure of the Liberal party to become a socialist party.[1] The Edwardian generation, like every generation, was imprisoned in its own environment. In the Liberal party of 1906 Asquith was comparatively a young man; it surprises us to note that he was born in 1852, went to Oxford in 1870, and entered Parliament in 1886. In other words, he learned his politics in the great days of Gladstone and Disraeli. Joseph Chamberlain in 1886 had just crossed the floor, and it was by no means certain, especially after the resignation of Lord Randolph Churchill, that he would not return. A period of years had to elapse, in which "Radical Joe" became an imperialist and the rich men of the Conservative party gave a few concessions for the sake of political unity, before he was completely absorbed. Meanwhile politics was little concerned with the condition of the people, for it was dominated by Home Rule, imperialist adventures, and the respective demands of the armed forces and the tax-payers. The Liberal party of the nineties was ill composed and psychologically disinclined to take up Joe's mantle. It was divided not in its approach to socialism but in its approach to imperialism.

Politicians like generals learn to fight the last war. The Edwardian Liberal party might have changed to a socialist party under pressure from terrible young men like Lloyd George and Winston Churchill,

but it was destroyed by the war of 1914–18.

In the second place, the psychological approach, even of a comparatively self-made man like Asquith, made most Liberals incapable of striking out on a new line. Asquith came from typical Liberal stock, "masters" in the woollen industry of Yorkshire; he was a day-boy at the City of London School; he won a scholarship to Balliol; and he went to the Bar in order to get into politics. He was one of Jowett's young men at Balliol and, like most of those young men, he was socially ambitious. He was apparently incapable of original ideas, and he hardly ever did anything original—marrying Margot Tennant as his second wife looks different, but he was probably well aware of the political value of her social prestige. Haldane, Morley and Grey were less conformist, but they were emotionally withdrawn from the East End.

*   *   *

Indeed the "paternalism" of the Conservatives and the experience of Joseph Chamberlain led many Unionists to take a more favourable view of working-class, and especially trade unionist, aspirations than many of the Liberals. Besides, it was good Unionist policy to "split the Liberal vote" by placating the Labour party.

Lloyd George was in a different category. He was a product of the lower class in agricultural, intensely Nonconformist Wales. He was very ambitious, the local boy who intended to make good; and he did make good, against much prejudice, by sheer ability, including much not very admirable cunning. Had he been born twenty years later he might possibly have become leader of the Labour party. As things were, he had to push his way in a Liberal party which was still intensely upper middle class. Unlike Asquith, he had not been made respectable by Oxford and the Bar; he had not married into the Liberal aristocracy; he was alien to the dominant Liberal elements by birth, lan-

[1] The word "Socialist" has developed a specialised meaning, the nationalisation of the means of production, distribution and exchange, thus leaving us without a word to express the idea, which every party has now to support, of a system of comprehensive social services. It is not an essential part of socialism, in the broader sense (indicated by the small letter), that the State should become the sole employer, since that is only one method of ensuring a national minimum standard of living. The word is of French origin and merely means social reform. Thus a "socialiste" is a "partisan d'un système de réformes sociales": Littré, *Dictionnaire de la langue française.* Cf. *Encyclopædia Britannica* (11th ed.), xxv, p. 301: "Socialism is that policy or theory which aims at securing by the action of the central democratic authority a better distribution, and in subordination thereto a better production, of wealth than now prevails." When first used in England, in the eighteen-twenties, socialism meant "social justice."

guage and upbringing. Even those who admired him, like Tom Jones,[2] thought he was a bit of a bounder. Since Disraeli became leader of the Conservative party and almost its patron saint it is impossible to say that Lloyd George could never have become leader of a Liberal party which capitalised the Liberal prejudices of the trade unions—which were still strong even after 1906—and absorbed the small Labour

party. Certainly he was far abler than Ramsay MacDonald. Had Asquith been removed by act of God, Lloyd George was enough of a careerist to suppress, in a larger "Lib-Lab" policy, his peculiar Welsh and Nonconformist prejudices; and indeed there were staunch Labour men who shared those prejudices. With Asquith in authority, Lloyd George could never secure genuine Liberal support; and before 1914 he looked rather to a coalition with the Conservatives than to a Liberal party founded on the support of the labour movement.

[2] A Welshman, deputy secretary of the cabinet, 1916–30, and biographer of Lloyd George. [EDITOR'S NOTE.]

Radicals Defeated in 1886

J. L. GARVIN

Chamberlain was fortunate in his biographer, James Louis Garvin (1868-
1947). An influential editor of *The Observer* for 34 years, a post he surrendered in 1942, he had a close association with Chamberlain, and shared
many of his views. A Liberal Imperialist and advanced social reformer, he
followed the radical leader in 1886, and later campaigned for his tariff
reforms. He lived to complete three volumns (1932-4) of an official biography.
Julian Amery has written volume four, and is expected to conclude the study
with a fifth. Garvin's sympathies for Chamberlain and his radical program in
1885-6 are shown in the following selection.

THE QUEEN's speech [August 1885] dispersing the House of Commons was read to almost empty benches. Journals and reviews were full of serious reflection. The epoch of middle-class Liberalism had passed; the signposts pointed to democracy. While the *Spectator* saw in Parnell, Chamberlain and Churchill the men of the new time, the *Economist* said that during the late Parliament the new Radicalism had been born, with Chamberlain for its "most prominent exponent." As for Radicals, many were declaring with Labouchere that when Mr. Gladstone withdrew from public life, "his mantle will descend upon Mr. Chamberlain, who must be our next Premier." This was the sentiment of the working class rank and file.

*   *   *

His brief [Chamberlain's] was ready in *The Radical Programme,* a collection and revision of articles which for nearly two years had been running through the *Fortnightly Review,* then edited by Escott, who succeeded John Morley. Earlier pages have shown how Chamberlain organised the articles in collaboration with Escott, who were the writers, and how, as he said, he "knocked about" some contributors like Frank Harris. The volume, in a scarlet cover, was issued with a preface from his pen and had a wider vogue than any catechism, of its kind in that age. He did not pledge himself to everything in it, but in the main it was his handbook. The preface ran:

The Reform Acts of 1885 have set the seal on the great change which the Reform Act of 1832 inaugurated.

The government of the people by the people, imperfectly recognised as the principle of the first attempt to improve the Parliamentary Representation, has been at last effectively secured by the two measures which together constitute the great achievement of Mr. Gladstone's second administration.

At last the majority of the nation will be represented by a majority of the House of Commons, and ideas and wants and claims which have been hitherto ignored in legislation will find a voice in Parliament, and will compel the attention of statesmen.

Radicalism, which has been the creed of the most numerous section of the Liberal party outside the House of Commons, will hence-

From J. L. Garvin, *The Life of Joseph Chamberlain,* II (London, 1933). Reprinted by permission of Macmillan & Co., Ltd., pp. 55–58, 83–85, 89–90, 154–155.

forth be a powerful factor inside the walls of the popular Chamber.

The stage of agitation has passed and the time for action has come.

There is need, therefore, for the attempt which is made in the following pages to compile a definite and practical programme for the Radical party.

It is a mistake to suppose that the objects of the advanced Liberals are simply destructive, for although the ground has to be cleared in many places, the new necessities of the time can only be fully met by constructive legislation.

New conceptions of public duty, new developments of social enterprise, new estimates of the natural obligations of the members of the community to one another, have come into view and demand consideration.

On this account, and without pledging myself to all the proposals contained in the following articles, I welcome their appearance, and commend them to the careful and impartial judgment of my fellow-countrymen.

Some weeks later he invited for the little book the earnest attention of the country and the fair consideration of his opponents. "I wish that some of those who on Tory platforms go about abusing their opponents without much knowledge would make themselves acquainted with the contents of that book. I do not suppose that they would agree with what it contains—they would not be Tories if they did—but at least they would see that there is nothing dangerous and nothing unconstitutional and nothing unjust in the great majority of the proposals made on behalf of the Radical party." It is doubtful whether Conservatives who followed this advice and looked well into the volume found much ease. The editor's introduction, every word of it settled in agreement with the statesman, expressed very well the spirit of the proposals:

They sound the death-knell of the *laissez-faire* system. . . . The goal towards which the advance will probably be made at an accelerated pace is that in the direction of which the legislation of the last quarter of a century has been tending—the intervention, in other words, of the State on behalf of the weak against the strong, in the interests of labour against capital, of want and suffering against luxury and ease.

These latter words went indeed to the heart of the matter.

*   *   *

In the sight of the enlarged democracy or at least of its labouring masses he [Chamberlain] stood out more than ever as Mr. Gladstone's successor. The sooner, many of them thought, the better.

*   *   *

This personal matter Chamberlain had not intended to raise. It occupied no large place in his thoughts, too positively engaged otherwise—engrossed by Radicalism and by the idea of democracy "with executive force and authority." He said at Warrington: "The great agitation which has set the seal upon popular government in this country is the work of the Radical party, which now constitutes the great majority of the Liberal party, and the 'armchair' politicians who looked on with indifference while we were bearing the heat and burthen of the day have no claim, and they have no power, to deprive us of the fruits of victory." Without guarantees for Radicalism he would not again serve under Gladstone or anyone. . . . The epilogue of his Radical crusade was delivered amongst his own people. He summed up:

Everywhere in the counties there is a great awakening; there is enthusiasm, expectation and hope. When I was in Wiltshire the other day, a gentleman told me that he had attended a meeting of Wiltshire labourers, and he was surprised by the quickness and intelligence with which they followed the speakers; and he said to a man who was standing by him, "How is it that these labourers understand politics so well?" "Oh," said the other, "it is because since they got the franchise they have thought of nothing else. They talk of it by day, they dream of it by night. It is positively sickening." Yes,

I daresay it is sickening to some of those old-fashioned Tories to see how those who were once their serfs are awakening to their new responsibilities and their new privileges. It will be still more sickening when the result of the election is known, for I do not hesitate to predict that if the towns do their duty there will be the greatest Liberal majority at the next election that the country has known during the last half-century.

And predominantly it would be a Radical majority. Of democracy and tomorrow this was his confident vision. We must now see what happened to it and him. Another mind had another vision and for a short time another will was to overpower his own.

* * *

On August 1, Mr. Gladstone wrote: "My dear Chamberlain . . . should you wish to see me I am quite open to you but with limited powers of speech." They met three days later in London. The conversation led to nothing of much mark, and chiefly left on the mind of the Radical visitor the pleasing impression that Gladstone was rather favourable to graduated taxation.

* * *

The ex-Premier then went to Norway to meditate more deeply both his strategy and his precautions. He was away for four weeks, and returned at the beginning of September to find the ranks of Liberalism thrown into disarray by dispute on the "unauthorised programme." That fact was by no means unfavourable to the chief condition of the "grand design" concerning Ireland—Gladstone's continued leadership. Chamberlain's campaign was in full swing; Hartington[1] in full protest. Between them Liberalism was in distraction and tumult. Yet there was a strange feature. While

[1] Marquess of Hartington (Eighth Duke of Devonshire after December, 1891) and leader of the Whigs or right-wing Liberals. [EDITOR'S NOTE.]

Gladstone stood on the whole with the Whigs on the social ground—where the leader of the Liberal Left and the spokesman of the Liberal Right were at open war —Chamberlain and Hartington were in unwonted agreement on the Irish Question; the Radical even the more trenchant of the two in spurning the summons to surrender when Parnell's speech at Dublin demanded in a legislative sense "National Independence." That speech was called "as bad as bad could be" by Gladstone himself. Who could decipher him?

Would the older leader still lead? Upon the answer everything depended. Had Gladstone then retired, the Liberal party, however strained within itself, could not have been shattered. Hartington saw clearly that if temporarily weakened by Whig secession it would be strongly reconstituted by the Radicals. Gladstone acquired the power to disrupt it because his renewed sway was thought by the Whig noblesse to be the only means for some further period of keeping Liberalism intact yet restricted to a moderate social policy. Had he not been for five years the Ulysses of accommodation? Had he not kept his Government together again and again when its dissensions seemed almost hopeless? But it was Gladstone after all who was to drive out the Whigs and the Radical leader too.

* * *

This chapter is meant to leave a mingling of impressions reflecting faithfully the unexampled confusions, amazements, perplexities, prevailing in these last two weeks of December. Chamberlain cries to Dilke (December 27), "What are we to do? This may mean isolation for a long time."

Upon resistance at any cost, if things come to the worst, he is bent. Already he is shaping and sharpening his weapons— every argument he was soon to wield in debate. So far he is clear, but only so far. At the same time he is lacerated by dread of the break with what he had most cared

for—with the mass of his party—with all
the affection, pride, allegiance, so recently
given him by the ranks of advanced
Liberalism. Some momentary contradictions are to the credit of his heart and his
head.

Not because his own inward resolve
wavers for a moment, but for tactical and
tactile reasons in connection with his
party, he throws out various and inconsistent schemes turning upon "ifs."

"If" we meant to concede a National
Parliament to Ireland, then let us federate
the whole United Kingdom by adopting
the American Constitution. "If" the more
one-sided plan is to be applied, then, to
diminish friction and danger, let us get
rid of Ireland altogether, reserving such
powers only as shall prevent that country
from becoming a base for foreign aggression against Great Britain. Using that idea
as a device to give pause to Gladstonians,
he did not for a moment conceive it as a
real alternative. The essence of his mind
just at this outset was expressed in a
simplifying phrase to Dilke: "(A)
National Councils; (B) Separation."
Home-Rule-All-Round, strong federalism
with State rights under one Supreme
Parliament—this he still holds to be by far
the best course; and that Parnell may be
forced to come to it if the Liberals refuse
to give more. But always he comes back
to his inmost conviction that nothing but
disaster incalculable can follow any attempt
to deal in a hurry with this revolutionising
business by means of a Liberal Govern-

ment dependent on Irish support in a manner certain to be regarded as ignominious
by the majority of the English people.
Gladstone and Parnell will not have his
solution. He will not have theirs.

Was he right? Before the answer can
be given with certainty the future must
yield up some of the secrets it still reserves
after nearly half a century.

We can only say that his policy would
have prevented Liberal disruption; ensured
the speedy beginnings of moderate Home
Rule; provided the best chance for a united
as well as a self-governing Ireland; while
creating for the whole United Kingdom,
as in the United States, a federal constitution ordered yet democratic. The Conservatives, by Chamberlain's policy of
"Keeping the Tories In" for a time, might
have been brought to co-operate in the
process just outlined. If Gladstone, according to his suggestions to Balfour, gravely
wished to bring the Conservatives to an
agreed measure of Irish self-government,
his best course would have been to hold
his hand and to allow the new parliamentary situation to develop before taking
office himself. This was Chamberlain's
desire.

In the present writer's opinion, Gladstone's retirement after the General
Election of 1885 would have been best for
the three great questions—the Irish question, the Social question, and the Imperial
question alike. Best even for Parnell as
well as for the Radical leader.

Liberals Healthy on Eve of War

TREVOR WILSON

Trevor Wilson, a New Zealander, and now Senior Lecturer in History at the
University of Adelaide in Australia, has written the only full-length study of
the Liberal collapse. Before expounding his own thesis—that the First World
War initiated a process of disintegration—Wilson undertakes to clear the
ground of adverse interpretations. He gives careful attention, as seen below,
to the view that Labor was already destroying the Liberal party by 1914.

I T IS COMMONLY believed that the
Liberal party began to fall well before
1914. I recall discussing this matter with
some fellow-undergraduates when I was
first becoming interested in the subject.
One of them set the ball rolling by asking
"When did the Liberal party reach the
point of no return?" (He was an American
student.) Their answers covered many
years. One considered the Liberal party
doomed from the time of the Home Rule
split in the 1880's; another from the
foundation of the Independent Labour
party in the 1890's, or anyway the Labour
Representation Committee in 1900; another from the election of Labour M.P.s in
1906; another from the political upheavals
of the period 1910-1914 ("The Strange
Death of Liberal England"). Thus to
satisfy every view about when and why
the Liberal party met its doom, one might
as well go back to the time when there was
a party bearing the name Liberal at all.

This temptation has been resisted. The
account given here is confined to the
period when the Liberal party was clearly
disintegrating. Such was not the case
before 1914. If the party passed through
troubled times between 1885 and 1905, its
electoral victories from 1906 to 1910 appeared to show it fully recovered. Between

1911 and 1914 it again encountered difficulties: Nonconformity, at least for the
moment, had passed its peak, the situation
in Ireland was full of menace, Labour was
talking of ending its alliance with the
Liberals, there was much industrial unrest,
and by-elections seemed to show that the
Liberals would lose the next election to
the Conservatives. All of these are reasons
for believing that the Liberal party might
soon have been out of office. They do not
show that it was doomed to near-extinction. The fact that Nonconformity was
losing ground did not mean that it might
not soon recover it. And although the Conservatives were capturing seats in by-elections, it was not certain that before long
they would capture office. There seemed
no limit to their folly during these years.
They had lost two elections in 1910, soon
after their prospects had begun to look rosy,
by encouraging the House of Lords to
wildly irresponsible conduct. In 1914 the
crisis in Ireland was acting to their advantage; but they might still have carried
their disregard for law and order over this
issue to a point which would shock
moderate opinion and lose them another
election.

The most menacing problem for the
Liberals before August 1914 was relations

From Trevor Wilson, *The Downfall of the Liberal Party 1914–1935* (London, 1966). Reprinted by
permission of Collins Publishers and Cornell University Press, pp. 15–17.

with Labour. The Liberal party contained a substantial element of wealthy businessmen, many of whom held individualistic views on economic matters and looked askance at the trade union movement; in Scotland, particularly, Liberal-Labour relations had for some years been awkward. To maintain a working alliance with Labour, the Liberals would probably have been obligated to shed some of these more "conservative" elements. But such a shedding process had occurred before without causing irrevocable disaster. The real danger to the Liberals was that in seeking to retain their "whigs" they might lose contact with Labour. Yet in 1914 this was not happening. The social reforming wing of the Liberal government was making the running. "Advanced" thinkers were still looking to Liberalism to implement their ideas. And Labour had put forward no major policy items which the Liberal party was unable to implement.

Nor in purely electoral terms was there any sign that Labour was supplanting the Liberals. In the general elections of 1910, and in by-elections from 1911 until the outbreak of war, Labour fared abysmally in contests with the Liberals. Twice in by-elections during these years Liberals contested Labour-held seats, and on both occasions Labour come bottom of the poll. Thus even in constituencies where Labour could not be dismissed as a "hopeless" party (because it happened to be in occupation), it could not hold its own against the Liberals. By and large, the Labour parliamentary party still existed in 1914 by Liberal indulgence—that is, because the Liberals deemed it advantageous to give Labour a free run against the Conservatives in certain seats. There is no way of knowing what would have happened before the war if Labour had set itself up in rivalry to the Liberals. On the basis of electoral evidence up to 1914, both would have suffered, but Labour would have fared much worse than the Liberals. Whether, in that event, Labour would have persisted in hopeless battles, or would have made a new (and probably more favorable) agreement with the Liberals, is a matter for speculation. It did not appear inevitable that Labour would persist in the former course.

Liberals in the Running before 1914

SAMUEL H. BEER

Agreeing with Trevor Wilson on the healthy state of the Liberals before 1914 is Samuel H. Beer, Professor of Government at Harvard University. A former Rhodes scholar and noted student of British politics, Beer emphasizes the cooperation between the Labour and Liberal parties before the war, and does not even exclude the possibility of a fusion which would make Labour a "socialistic, though not Socialist" wing of the Liberal party. As with Wilson he believes that the First World War was responsible for a shift in political power which doomed the Liberals.

THE LABOUR PARTY has its great place in the history of British Socialism. But it also has a place in the history of British pressure politics. Knowing what the party later became, one may be tempted to read its later into its earlier character, and so to give undue prominence to Socialist influences during its first years. In trying to characterize the party as a political formation at that time, it is helpful to look at it as part of the new pattern of politics that emerged between the Third Reform Act and the First World War.

The key element in this new pattern was the organized interest group based on an occupational stratum of what had become a highly industrialized economy. A few examples may be mentioned. As previously observed, the railway politics of the late nineteenth century had been much affected by the rise of nationwide associations of manufacturers and traders. In general, employers were developing organizations not only for economic purposes, but also for political action. In the last twenty years of the century, trade associations began to appear in substantial numbers and in 1898 the Employers Parliamentary Council, an interindustry organization for representing business interests

before Parliament and Government, was set up,[1] although British business did not find lasting and effective agents of political action until the establishment of the Federation of British Industries and the National Union of Manufacturers during the First World War. From its beginnings in 1870, the National Union of Teachers,[2] the agent chiefly of the elementary school teachers, took to pressure politics, as did the associations of their more genteel competitors from the secondary schools. The ancient landed interest itself gradually turned to organized political action, landowners taking the lead in the first phase, which began with the founding of the Central Chamber of Agriculture in 1865,[3] while farmers took the initiative in the

[1] Frank Bealey and Henry Pelling, *Labour and Politics 1900–1906: A History of the Labour Representation Committee* (London, 1958), p. 13; S. E. Finer, "The Federation of British Industries," *Political Studies*, Vol. IV, No. 1 (February, 1956), p. 61.

[2] See Asher Tropp, *The School Teachers: The Growth of the Teaching Profession in England and Wales from 1800 to the Present Day* (New York, 1957).

[3] See Alfred H. H. Matthews, *Fifty Years of Agricultural Politics: The History of the Central Chamber of Agriculture 1865–1915* (London, 1915).

From Samuel H. Beer, *Modern British Politics* (London, 1965). Reprinted by permission of Faber and Faber Ltd., and Alfred A. Knopf, pp. 109–112, 124–125, 140–141, 143–144.

second phase with the organization of the National Farmers Union in 1908.[4]

This is not the place to relate the political history of these bodies. It will be touched on only to note the many similarities with the political behavior of trade unions. The Parliamentary Committee of the T.U.C. [Trade Union Congress] on behalf of organized labor as a whole, as well as individual unions on behalf of their respective memberships, sought to influence ministers and M.P.'s by standard lobbying techniques, backing up their powers of persuasion with meetings calculated to affect public opinion and with attempts to pledge candidates to the support of desired measures. So also did these other organized groups of producers. Moreover, other interest groups sought some sort of direct representation in Parliament. Economic strata, such as landowners and businessmen, which consisted of persons with wealth and social position, enjoyed direct representation simply from the presence in Parliament of "interested" M.P.'s who themselves owned land or engaged in business. For this reason there was less need for these groups to turn to organization for the purpose of influencing Westminster and Whitehall or winning representation. Still, both the Central Chamber of Agriculture and the Employers Parliamentary Council had members in the House who helped with legislative matters.

Organizations of the less-advantaged groups in the economy, however, turned most readily to the new methods and pushed them farther. For instance, they sought direct representation by sponsored M.P.'s—members who were ready to advocate the views of the organization in the House and who in turn received a subsidy for their election expenses and perhaps also, as in the case of trade union M.P.'s, maintenance while they were in Parliament. While the best-known examples are the sponsored M.P.'s of trade unions during their Lib–Lab phase, the N.U.T. [National Union of Teachers] also successfully used this device and it was imitated in the plans of the Farmers Union.

A further extension of the new pressure politics was the attempt to turn a number of "interested" M.P.'s into a bloc that would act independently of the two major parties on questions of direct interest to the outside organization. In 1900 the teachers achieved this on a modest scale with their three sponsored M.P.'s, two Liberals and one Conservative. The Central Chamber of Agriculture attempted something of the sort in its establishment of a bipartisan agricultural committee in the House. The Farmers Union similarly hoped to create from its pledged and sponsored M.P.'s a bloc that could manipulate the balance of power on agricultural issues before the House and, while no "direct representatives of the Union" were elected until 1922, some sixty-eight M.P.'s pledged to support the N.F.U. program were returned in 1910.[5]

Likewise, during the Lib–Lab phase of trade union politics, which began with the election of MacDonald and Burt in 1874, the relationship of Labour members with the Liberal Party consisted in "a system by which you cordially cooperate with your friends, whilst reserving to yourself, should need arise, your own independence of action."[6] The Lib–Labs attempted to act in unison, an effort that was promoted by the Parliamentary Committee of the T.U.C. that met with them to discuss parliamentary action, and by such actions as the formation in 1899 of a group of eight Lib–Lab M.P.'s "to watch closely the agenda paper of the House of Commons, in order to be prepared when labour questions were likely to be under discussion."[7] Indeed, they showed their independence not only on labor questions, but also at times on

[4] See Peter Self and Herbert J. Storing, *The State and the Farmer* (London, 1962).

[5] *Ibid.*, pp. 42–3.
[6] Henry Broadhurst, as quoted in Bealey and Pelling, *op. cit.*, p. 188.
[7] T.U.C. Report 1899, quoted in Bealey and Pelling, *op. cit.*, p. 185.

such "political" questions as the South African war.

The sectionalism of the trade union movement, however, impaired their cohesion. In 1894 the Webbs, referring to the trade union movement, wrote:

the basis of the association of these million and a half wage-earners is primarily sectional in its nature. They come together, and contribute their pence, for the defence of their interests as Boilermakers, Miners, Cotton-spinners, and not directly for the advancement of the whole working class. . . . The vague general Collectivism . . . [of the salaried officers of the unions] has hitherto got translated into practical proposals only in so far as it can be expressed in projects for the advantage of a particular trade.

As a result, they continued, the question whether it was possible to "counteract the fundamental sectionalism of Trade Union organisation" and "to render the Trade Union world . . . an effective political force in the State" was "the most momentous question of contemporary politics."[8]

At the same time, the pull of party was strong and the Lib–Labs sat as Liberals and usually voted with the main body of the party. The organized agricultural interest was also confronted with that problem. In spite of their efforts to lift agricultural questions above party politics, both the C.C.A. and the N.F.U. found their representatives almost entirely among Conservatives on whom the demands of party usually overrode the claims of the agricultural interest. Disappointment with the tactic of the independent bloc led some sections of the C.C.A. to press for a bolder initiative when in 1907–8 a fairly strong move was initiated to set up an Agricultural Party. The local chambers, it is said, welcomed the proposal, but the C.C.A.'s governing body, in which M.P.'s were numerous, killed it with amendments.[9]

The trade unions successfully achieved this further extension of pressure politics—which agriculture was unable to attempt—when they established and maintained the Labour Party. That event constituted not so much a change of goals as a change of tactics. The new tactics meant that the Labour M.P.'s would have a solidarity that the Lib–Labs had been unable to achieve. In particular, they were to be members not of either major party, but of a distinct group that had the power to make binding decisions on its own policy. As before, however, the goals were primarily defined by "the direct interests of labour."

*   *   *

One is tempted to say that . . . [the] concerns of the Labour Party reflect nothing more than a straightforward, utilitarian politics of economic self-interest, untainted by ideology or social philosophy. But what an individual or organization takes to be its "interest" is not an immediate datum of experience. It results from an interpretation of that experience and in this interpretation some broader perspective—perhaps vague, perhaps ambiguous—plays an important part. The principal measures advocated by the Labour Party in these years could still be justified on the premises of Radicalism and were so conceived by the bulk of the party in Parliament and the country.[10] These measures consisted of state action not merely to eliminate conditions judged bad, but also to create conditions judged good, the state itself sometimes providing these conditions by means of services that might involve redistribution of wealth. Such intervention, however, was piecemeal: it aimed to correct particular grievances and was usually instigated by the pressure of some particular social group. It certainly constituted no attempt to assert governmental guidance of the economy as a whole or to change fundamentally its individualist and capitalist character.

---

[8] *History of Trade Unionism*, new ed. (London, 1920), pp. 678–9.
[9] Matthews, *op. cit.*, p. 340.

[10] For the Radical conception of policy in contrast with the Socialist conception, see above, Ch. III, 79–82.

The bulk of the party, in short, shared a general frame of thought and values within which it carried on its politics of interest, and this perspective could still be fitted into the ideology of Liberal Radicalism. Ramsay MacDonald may well have been exaggerating (for obvious tactical reasons), but it is notable that he could say, while negotiating the *entente* of 1906 with Herbert Gladstone, not only that the majority of the members of the L.R.C.[11] had hitherto worked with the Liberals and wished to continue, but also that the L.R.C. candidates were "in almost every case earnest Liberals who [would] support a Liberal Government."[12]

And in fact the Labour M.P.'s did more than merely serve the immediate interests of trade unions. They also joined enthusiastically in support of the other Radical reforms of Campbell-Bannerman's and Asquith's great "New Deal" Governments. "The Labour Party," wrote Lowell in 1908, ". . . professes to be wholly independent of all other parties, but really agrees with, and is inclined to support, the Liberals on matters that do not touch the special interests of Labour."[13] In the 1906 and 1908 sessions, for instance, a majority of Labour M.P.'s voted with the Government tellers in 89.0% and 84.0% respectively of all divisions. This was not strange. On the whole, these Labour M.P.'s ardently shared the Liberal commitment to Free Trade, Nonconformity, and Home Rule. They adhered to the Radicals' antimilitarism and anti-imperialism and with them championed democracy against aristocracy. They sided with the Government in its effort to amend the Education Act of 1902 and in its equally futile effort for temperance reform. They could vote solidly against the Government in support of their own Unemployed Workmen bill.[14] They sought to exploit their tactic of solidarity by bargaining with the Government, as when in 1911 MacDonald promised Lloyd George that the party would support his National Insurance bill and in return obtained state payment of M.P.'s.[15] But they avoided broad challenges of the Liberal Party at the polls and in Parliament worked with them to bring about a reformist achievement that has been compared with 1832 and 1945.

* * *

In view of the leaders' public adherence to independence, it is not strange that they felt obliged to conceal the *entente* of 1906 from the membership. Such electoral arrangements have often been the road to fusion. Nor did the agreement of 1906 mark a temporary and exceptional tactic. In practice, Labour continued to refrain from offering a broad electoral challenge to the Liberals during the prewar period.

It is hardly a universal law of political behavior that when two parties follow a tactic such as that represented by the *entente* of 1906, they must have in common some bond of ideology, or at least not be divided by opposing ideologies. Still, such cooperation is greatly facilitated if the allies belong to the same political tendency. MacDonald suggested as much when, in the 1906 negotiations, he made his only slightly mendacious statement to Herbert Gladstone that the L.R.C. candidates could be regarded as "earnest Liberals." So long as Labour's purposes were simply those of trade union politics, framed in the broad terms of Radical ideology, the independence of the party was still seriously in doubt. Indeed, there remained the real possibility that it might become simply a wing of a more socialistic, though not Socialist, Liberal Party.

[11] Labour Representation Committee. Formed in 1900 of a number of Socialist societies and trade unions for the purpose of securing Labour representation in Parliament. Later became the Labour party. [EDITOR'S NOTE.]
[12] Quoted in Philip P. Poirier, *The Advent of the British Labour Party* (New York, 1958) p. 186.
[13] A. L. Lowell, *The Government of England*, new ed. (New York, 1924) Vol. II, p. 41.

[14] Division 41 *H. C.Deb.*, 1908.
[15] Henry Pelling, *A Short History of the Labour Party* (London, 1961) p. 27.

*   *   *

Some have tried to explain the Labour Party's break with the Liberals as a fairly simple economic calculation: the Liberals had failed to represent the interests and remedy the grievances of the working class, and more specifically, the organized working class of the trade unions. Hence, it is said, disillusioned with the old cooperative strategy and the attempt to remedy their grievances within capitalism, the unions concluded that only a change in system would satisfy their needs. This has been an explanation which Socialists have stressed. In the debate of 1923, for instance, Snowden claimed that although there had been an improvement in the material condition of the working class between 1850 and 1874, the period 1874–1908 had witnessed a relative and absolute decline.

There is indeed evidence of both a relative and absolute decline in the condition of the working class before World War I. In 1910 real wages were substantially below what they had been in 1900, and they did not begin to rise until 1914. Moreover, since the end of the century the share of the national income going to wage-earners had fallen considerably.[16] These material factors no doubt contributed to the labor unrest that disturbed industrial relations just before the outbreak of war and on which the Syndicalists capitalized. But this turn toward direct action by some trade unionists does not correlate with a shift toward Socialism in the unions generally. They, as we have noted, remained hostile. Indeed, when judged in the light of what trade unions and the Labour Party were demanding in the sphere of government action, the tactic of cooperation had been remarkably successful. There had been friction with Liberal Governments and delays in the satisfaction of Labour's demands. But in sum the corpus of social reform enacted in the half dozen years or so after 1906 constituted an achievement that has often been compared with the results of 1832 and 1945. Not only did Liberal Governments and the Liberal Party outside Parliament adopt proposals originating with Labour and the unions; in important instances the Liberals took the initiative in conceiving and proposing basic measures. Hugh Dalton recalls: "The Liberals, indeed, were making the running in those years."

[16] Ben C. Roberts, *The Trade Union Congress, 1886–1921* (Cambridge, Mass., 1958) p. 233.

Decline of Nonconformist Conscience

JOHN F. GLASER

Historians agree that English Nonconformity was absorbed into the Liberal party in the 1860's and 70's, and gave Liberal politics a moral appeal and cutting edge. Some have maintained that all periods of religious vigor are periods of political radicalism. If this thesis is accepted, it is logical to expect that a decline of Nonconformity late in the century would usher in an age of political conservatism. John F. Glaser, Professor of History at Ripon College, Wisconsin, has gone beyond this to draw a direct correlation between a decline in Nonconformity and the collapse of the Liberal party. His interpretation, reprinted below, was first presented at a session of the American Historical Association in December, 1954.

By 1914 the Liberalism which had been the animating force of Victorian England and which experienced a vigorous renascence in Edwardian England seemed to have spent itself, unable to cope with the problems besetting Britain on the eve of the First World War. An essential part of this greatness and decline of Liberalism was the greatness and decline of English Nonconformity—the Protestant sects dissenting from the Church of England.[1] During the nineteenth century Nonconformists had been characterized by religious vitality and political strength, forming what Gladstone called "the backbone of British Liberalism." Seemingly more powerful than ever before at the beginning of the twentieth century, they contributed to and shared in the Liberal party triumph of 1906. Yet by 1914 it was apparent that Nonconformity, like Liberalism, had faltered; by the 1920's its religious vitality had markedly weakened and its political influence was negligible. It is the purpose of this article to examine the crisis of English Liberalism in terms of the crisis of the Nonconformist conscience. The theme is significant because Liberalism — whether regarded as a political party, an economic creed, or a frame of mind—throughout its history was closely related to Nonconformity, from which it drew constant spiritual nourishment and material strength.

The term "Nonconformist conscience" first came into popular usage as a by-product of the Parnell affair in 1890. It was largely owing to Nonconformist pressure that Gladstone repudiated Parnell, a convicted adulterer and perjurer, and thus ensured his fall as leader of the Irish Parliamentary party. As the Methodist preacher Hugh Price Hughes thundered: "We stand immovably on this eternal rock; what is morally wrong can never be politically right." Though the Nonconformist

[1] English Nonconformity embraces a wide theological spectrum, including Congregationalists, Baptists, Methodists, Presbyterians, Quakers, and Unitarians. In this article I shall follow the customary practice of using the collective terms "Nonconformity," "Dissent," and "Free Churches" interchangeably to designate all the Protestant groups outside of the Church of England. "Dissent," the standard term in the eighteenth century, had become somewhat old-fashioned by the middle of the nineteenth century, when it was superceded by "Nonconformity" in popular usage. The modern Nonconformist preference for "Free Churches" may be dated officially from the formation of the National Free Church Council in 1892.

From John F. Glaser, "English Nonconformity and the Decline of Liberalism," in the *American Historical Review*, vol. LXIII, No. 2, 1958. Reprinted by permission, pp. 352–363.

conscience became best known as the custodian of a censorious personal morality, it stood for much more than that narrow aspect of Puritanism; it was the "insistence upon the authority of moral principle in all matters of public policy." In the broadest sense, the Nonconformist conscience embraced the whole of the Nonconformist political outlook.

In the nineteenth century this outlook was conditioned by three factors: the strict moral code and humanitarian zeal inculcated by Evangelicalism, the bitter sense of grievance engendered by the civil disabilities and social discrimination suffered by Dissenters, and the middle-class character of Nonconformity. The division between "church" and "chapel" cut deep into the everyday life of Victorian England, so that Nonconformists "grew up in the centre of the national life a separate and peculiar people." Yet the Evangelical revival had made these chapel-folk strong in numbers and energy, and they belonged predominantly to that middle class which was rising to economic power with the industrial revolution and to political power with the changes following the Reform Act of 1832. "Political Dissent," the movement for religious equality, had as its natural ally the individualistic Liberalism of the Manchester School. Attacking landed and Anglican Conservatism, the agitations for free trade and free church went hand in hand.

Both Nonconformity and Radicalism found their strength in the commercial and industrial centers of provincial England. In those flourishing cities the leading members of the Nonconformist chapels were the local captains of industry, the spearheads of muncipal reform, and the magnates of the local Liberal party. Nonconformist families such as the Rathbones and Holts of Liverpool, the Chamberlains and Cadburys of Birmingham, the Peases and Backhouses of Darlington, the Salts and Illingworths of Bradford, the Baineses and Kitsons of Leeds, formed an urban governing class which, through intermarriage and business and political associations, had national ramifications. Nonconformity instilled in them a strong sense of public as well as private duty. Jeremiah Colman, the Norwich mustard manufacturer, wrote his future wife shortly before their marriage in 1856: "Talents consecrated to God are what the world and the Church wants.... I hope we shan't live an idle selfish existence, for I am sure it won't be a happy one if we do, and we must guard against it. Influence, position and wealth are not given for nothing, and we must try and use them as we should wish at the last we had done." In the course of the century the Nonconformist ministry increasingly turned from unworldly pietism to preach the doctrine that political responsibility was a religious duty. R. W. Dale of Birmingham insisted: "In a country like this, where the public business of the state is the private duty of every citizen, those who decline to use their political power are guilty of treachery both to God and to man."

Dale's activity in municipal and national Liberal politics was in striking contrast to the strictly religious interests of his longtime predecessor at Carrs Lane Chapel, John Angell James. This change was typical of orthodox Nonconformists, and it was accompanied by an increasing strain in their relations with their seemingly natural religious allies, the Evangelicals in the Church of England. During the 1860's there was a growing breach between the Evangelicals and the Dissenters. This was partly because many leading Nonconformists, such as Dale, had come into closer symypathy with the tolerant spirit of the Broad Churchmen while the Low Churchmen held their Evangelical orthodoxy with rigidity and even intolerance. The chief source of difference, however, was political, for, "as a rule, the Evangelicals were staunch upholders of what was called 'The Establishment,' and were almost without exception Conservatives."

The later 1860's and the 1870's brought an intensification of the Liberalism of Nonconformity. The Reform Act of 1867 and the emergence of a Liberal party led by Gladstone and blessed by Bright created conditions which drew Nonconformists more fully into the arena of national politics. The harvest of individualistic Liberalism had its fruits for political Dissent in the abolition of compulsory church-rates, the disestablishment of the Irish Church, and the removal of religious tests at Oxford and Cambridge. Though it originally precipitated a Nonconformist revolt, the Education Act of 1870 proved favorable to Nonconformist interests. Disestablishment of the Church of England was in the air in the 1870's. The Liberal party increasingly became a vehicle for humanitarian and moral causes in which even formerly nonpolitical Dissenters were interested—peace, temperance, repeal of the Contagious Diseases Acts.

Above all, Gladstone approached politics with a moral passion which had an almost idolatrous appeal to Dissenters of all sects and social strata. As earlier with Irish disestablishment and later with Home Rule, Nonconformists in the late 1870's made up the New Model Army of Gladstone's crusade against Bulgarian atrocities and Disraelian imperialism. The Eastern question formed a turning point in Nonconformist as well as English politics. The Nonconformist conscience became one with the national conscience as interpreted by the High Churchman Gladstone. "It is too commonly believed that 'political Dissent' means nothing more nor less than antagonism to the Establishment," wrote J. G. Rogers, a prominent Congregational minister and Liberal politician.

It really means the subordination of politics to Christian principles. One result of this would, in the judgment of Nonconformists, be the removal of all invidious distinctions resting on the ground of religious opinion, but the principle is of much wider application. It covers the entire area of international relations, and here Mr. Gladstone is recognized by the Nonconformists as one of the very few statesmen who feel that the law of Christ is to govern nations as well as individuals.

By 1880 Nonconformity was substantially absorbed into the Liberal party. Even the ancient conservatism of Wesleyan Methodism—never a part of traditional "political Dissent"—was giving way to active Liberalism. At this high tide of political solidarity and enthusiasm in the chapels, the leading Nonconformist newspaper declared:

Since the beginning of the century . . . it is certain that Britain has, in the intervals of her blindness, had some inspiring visions of the kingdom of justice one day to be established among men, and it is not to be denied that, taken broadly, the Liberal party has striven to follow the fiery pillar of conscience into this promised land. Like all human combinations it has had its good and evil, its truth and fallacy, its times of glory and disgrace. . . . But, speaking generally, it has striven to be "the party of Christ" . . . the party of moral principle as against that of selfish and corrupt interests, the party of peace as against that of violence, the party of popular improvement and reform as against that of resistance to progress, the party of justice as against that of despotic force or social disorder.

And the backbone of this party has been—to speak historically, without partisan reference [i.e., to Nonconformity]—the religious Protestantism and Puritanism of England. For a very good reason, because a party whose object it is to rule men's actions by a moral principle in legislation and government derives its force from conscience, and from the omnipotence which is behind it. . . . The strength of the Liberal party is, and always has been, in the force of individual and social conscience. It is a power which, like a mighty river in flood, must eventually carry everything before it, since it is in the nature of right to win at last.

If "the party of conscience" was much like a "secular church," certain of the Nonconformist churches tended to acquire the attributes of "political caucuses." The caucus had, in fact, been born among Birmingham Dissenters. But in fusing with the Liberal party, in acquiring the political habit, Nonconformity became more exposed to the fissures which increasingly cleft that party from the 1880's to the First

World War. The bulk of the Nonconformists—and especially the Nonconformist ministry—accepted Gladstone's view of
Irish Home Rule as a moral issue, but an
influential minority followed Chamberlain
and Bright, Dale and Spurgeon, into Liberal Unionism. At the turn of the century,
another imperial issue, the Boer War, split
Dissent more drastically. In both cases,
political division entailed some dissension
within the churches. Of special significance
was the personal tragedy of Dr. Dale, probably the finest representative of Victorian
Nonconformity. The bitterness engendered
by Home Rule caused him to withdraw
not only from the pro-Gladstonian Congregational Union in 1888 but also almost
entirely from public work. His disillusionment led him to oppose the formation of
the potentially political Free Church
Councils in 1892 and to warn against the
organized interference of churches in
politics.

Of all the issues which divided Nonconformists, it was socialism which had the
most fateful influence on Nonconformity
as a political and religious force. It is well
known that the Nonconformist chapel provided one of the seed-beds of the Labour
movement, and that Nonconformity helped
to awaken the working classes to political
consciousness. The early "Lib–Lab" M.P.'s,
such as Burt, Broadhurst, Arch, Abraham,
and Pickard, were usually Dissenters and
often lay preachers, and they shared the
predilections of Nonconformist Radicalism.
Nor were middle-class Nonconformists reluctant to modify extreme individualism to
meet the demands of municipal efficiency,
notably in Birmingham under Chamberlain's leadership, or the challenges of working-class misery, dramatized by another
Dissenter in *The Bitter Cry of Outcast
London*. But the spread of socialist ideas
and the appearance of an Independent
Labour party in the 1890's posed a dilemma
which neither Nonconformity nor Liberalism was ultimately able to solve. Middle
class Nonconformists were torn between,
on the one hand, humanitarianism and traditional alliance with the working classes
and, on the other hand, self-interest and
traditional individualism. There was an
unbridgeable chasm between Dr. Clifford's
vision of "fellowship with Socialists" and
what Joseph Chamberlain once called "the
decorous timidity of prosperous Dissent."
The leading London Liberal paper probably reflected the attitude of the typical
middle-class Dissenter, as it certainly did
of Gladstone, in not distributing its enthusiasm equally between the East End docker
and the Bulgarian peasant. Despite attempts by some ministers to preach a gospel of "Social Christianity," it seems just to
conclude that Nonconformity, on the
whole, was and remained basically individualistic.

These tensions within Nonconformity
helped to give the Liberal party its ambiva-
lent attitude toward social and economic
questions. In the crucial decade of the
1890's the failure of Liberalism to accom-
modate itself to working-class aspirations
was partly owing to the key position of provincial Nonconformists in the party. In
the North—especially in the West Riding
of Yorkshire—the local Liberal leaders, who
were usually Nonconformists, were often
large employers of labor. As a result, the
Liberal party appeared to be committed to
the point of view of the employers as
opposed to that of the employed. Bradford,
long a stronghold of Nonconformist Liberalism, is a classic example of the resulting tensions. The M.P. for West Bradford
was Alfred Illingworth, rich worsted spin-
ner, ardent Gladstonian, and old-time Nonconformist Radical of national prominence.
In the General Election of 1892 he was
opposed by an Independent Labour candidate, Ben Tillett, who attacked him as a
capitalist and employer. Though Tillett
was himself a Nonconformist and had
many Nonconformist supporters, organized
Nonconformity rallied to the cause of
Illingworth, who won the three-cornered
race by a narrow margin. A few months
later the outraged Bradford Labourites
formed a Labour Church, drawing some

members from the Dissenting chapels and from those with Dissenting backgrounds. And before the next General Election Illingworth retired from public life, disgusted with what he regarded as the Liberal party's retreat from individualism on economic issues.

Although Nonconformity was weakened by political divisions over socialism and imperialism, it helped to commit the Liberal party to causes which were becoming increasingly uncongenial and even alien to large sections of the new democracy. Liberalism in the 1890's appeared to many working-class voters as a Crotchet Castle, from which dreary teetotaling Dissenters launched raids on pubs, music halls, and politicians cited in divorce cases. In the Parnell affair, Nonconformists were simply defending the universal moral code of older Victorians, but the growing secularism and hedonism of English society was increasingly isolating puritanical Nonconformity. A conscience which criticized Lord Rosebery's horse racing and which considered "the three deadly enemies of England" to be "drink, impurity, and gambling" was not wholly in touch with what the *Christian World* hopefully called middle-class Puritanism's "newly-organised allies in the army of labour." It was, indeed, the Liberal government's unpopular bills for local veto on the sale of intoxicating liquors which helped to bring on the disastrous Liberal defeat in the General Election of 1895.

When the Liberals finally returned to office ten years later, they were aided by the wave of Nonconformist agitation against the Balfour government's Education Act of 1902. Free Churchmen of all political camps—Gladstonian Home Rulers and Liberal Unionists, pro-Boers and Liberal Imperialists, old-fashioned Radicals and I.L.P. socialists—united against this measure, which they denounced as endowing Anglican schools and putting a hardship on Nonconformist children in "single-school" areas. Dr. Clifford, the prominent Baptist minister whose political career extended from Chartism to Fabianism, led a

passive resistance movement in which many Nonconformists refused to pay school rates, preferring the martyrdom of prison or distraint upon their goods. This rebellion, blessed by the Liberal leadership, was the first and mildest of the revolts against lawful authority which rocked Britain before 1914. While the agitation against the Education Act seemed to show the power of Nonconformity, it made organized Nonconformity more political than ever before, and modern Free Churchmen are unanimous in condemning the wisdom of passive resistance, with its "cheapening of conscience by making it a "matter of faction."

In retrospect, this last stand of Nonconformity was an artificial resurgence. The seeming strength of Dissent was illusory; its very prosperity concealed an inner weakness. Despite outward signs of vitality, the number of those who regularly attended Nonconformist services steadily declined during the years before the First World War. The falling off was especially marked among the educated and the young. The saying that "a carriage never goes to a meeting-house for three generations" expressed an ancient truth of English social history. But the last decades of the nineteenth century and the first of the twentieth saw an acceleration of the familiar process by which the upper stratum of Dissent was absorbed into an Anglican and Conservative upper class—a loss no longer accompanied by compensating accessions from the classes below. The full opening of the older universities to Nonconformists in the 1870's opened the way to professional careers and opportunities hitherto inaccessible and hastened the escape of many young nonconformists from what Matthew Arnold called "the prison of Puritanism."

At the beginning of the twentieth century the Nonconformist *haute bourgeoisie* was losing the local influence which had distinguished it throughout the Victorian era. Through the growth of limited liability companies and outside management, the expanding family firms were abandoning their patriarchal character, with the personal bond between employer and employed. Municipal government could less often rely on the services of the old Nonconformist governing families, partly because these were being edged out by the new working-class democracy and partly because wealth was taking them into the ranks of the landed gentry or an indifferent rentier class. This was a phenomenon lamented by Beatrice Webb, who observed in 1899:

Munificent public work has been done at Liverpool by some of the wealthy Unitarian families, but these families are petering out, and the sons are not worthy of the fathers. Whether this is inevitable to all families, or the bad effect of two or three generations of luxury, I do not know. The present generation of rich folk want to enjoy themselves, find nothing to resist, no class or creed interest to fight for, so that they have ceased to consider anything but their pleasures.

Nonconformity had, indeed, become rich and was more than ever limited to the prosperous middle class. The passive resistance movement notwithstanding, "militant witness-bearing" was a thing of the past. Dr. Fairbairn complained in 1897: "It is perhaps harder to be a Nonconformist today than it has ever been in the history of England. The very decay of the disabilities from which our fathers suffered has made it harder to us than it was to them to dissent." More bitter was the assertion of a Nonconformist minister writing anonymously in 1909: "Nonconformity is not, it must be confessed, in the way of making saints. That is a secret which it has somehow lost. Its whole atmosphere is not the atmosphere wherein sainthood grows." He attributed this "loss of distinctly spiritual power" to Nonconformity's exclusive absorption in "political activity for political ends."

This sense of spiritual loss, admitted by the few, was accompanied by a more general feeling of political frustration. Had the Nonconformists delivered their conscience into the keeping of the National Liberal Federation? Had Dr. Dale been a prophet without honor in his warning that "the interference of organised churches with organised political societies has proved after all a false method of effecting the great objects of the Christian gospel"? The fact that after 1906 almost two hundred Free Churchmen were sitting in the House of Commons and that the Liberal front bench was to a marked degree Nonconformist in origin reflected the social complexion of Liberalism rather than the power of Nonconformity. Nor could that formidable phalanx force a new Education Bill, a Licensing Bill, or Welsh disestablishment through the House of Lords. The years after 1906 were years of disappointment and frustration for Free Churchmen. The failure of three Liberal ministers in their attempts to redress educational grievances was especially galling. "Some of us felt at the time that they did not try very hard," a leading Congregational preacher recalled after some thirty years had passed. Though supporting the Liberals against the Lords in the second General Election of 1910, W. R. Nicoll, the editor of the *British Weekly* and a personal friend of Lloyd George, privately admitted that "politicians on either side have done nothing for us."

On the eve of the war, Nonconformity, like official Liberalism, was politically exhausted and divided and hesitant as to the future. The issues in which Nonconformists were peculiarly interested, such as education and Welsh disestablishment, were only surface irritants outside of Wales. The old demand for disestablishment of the Church of England had all but disappeared. Temperance and other moral reforms associated with the Nonconformist conscience were even less popular and less representative of English opinion than they had been twenty years earlier. The so-called "middle-class morality" was being challenged not only by Shavian wit but by social practice. Religion no longer held the primary place in the lives of most Englishmen. For religious people, the vital issue was not church vs. chapel, but Christianity vs. unbelief. Dissent no longer carried with it a significant burden of legal or social disability. This emancipation of Nonconformists was a triumph of the Liberalism whose root was "respect for the dignity and worth of the individual." But when the iron went out of the soul of Nonconformity—when Dissent ceased to dissent—the robust vitality of traditional Liberalism was weakened.

The Liberal government, which had come into office on the old issues of free trade and church vs. chapel, attempted to meet the problems of the new century with collectivistic measures at home and alliances abroad. Though they showed a constructive vigor, these departures from the Gladstonian faith left many Liberals uncomfortable survivors from the Victorian past. Sir Edward Grey's foreign policy, in particular, evoked exasperated protests from the Liberal press and provincial Liberalism. More significant, from 1910 on the government had to lead a country paralyzed by factional disputes unprecedented since the 1830's. The revolt of the Conservatives over the Lloyd George budget and the Parliament Bill, the rise of syndicalism and the spread of strikes, the fury of the militant suffragettes, the defiance of Ulster and the threat of civil war in Ireland over the Home Rule Bill—all were rending the fabric of British society on the eve of the First World War. These struggles posed problems and involved methods with which Liberalism, based on government by discussion, was neither accustomed to deal nor able to cope. The coming of the war freed the Asquith government from these ordeals, but it added a new burden under which Liberalism collapsed. The war completed the undermining of the secure world in which Liberalism had performed its work. As has been seen, however, even before 1914 the decline of Nonconformity had as an inevitable consequence the decline of Liberalism. The ebbing of the Nonconformist conscience entailed the gradual loss of the Liberal party's practical political strength and, more important, the loss of the religious ethos and moral passion which had distinguished English Liberalism in its creative golden age.

Conscious Rejection of Liberal Values

GEORGE DANGERFIELD

George Dangerfield, born in England and now an American citizen living in California, has produced prize-winning volumes on American and English history. His gracefully written account of the mental and social state of England on the eve of the First World War has influenced many historians, and its thesis is now found in many standard textbooks. Students are advised to resist the charm of the style in order to examine critically the argument which Dangerfield presents.

THE RIGHT HONORABLE Herbert Henry Asquith was enjoying a brief holiday on the Admiralty yacht *Enchantress*, bound for the Mediterranean on some pleasant excuse of business. He had put in at Lisbon to dine with King Manoel of Portugal, and his reception in this precarious capital had been very gratifying. The *Enchantress* then headed for Gibraltar, and was rolling its valuable political freight about halfway between that rock and Cadiz when news was received that Edward VII was seriously ill. The yacht turned hurriedly and made for home, and was well past the Bay of Biscay when, at three in the morning of May 7, 1910, a second message arrived. "I am deeply grieved to inform you that my beloved father the King passed away peacefully at a quarter to twelve tonight (the 6th). GEORGE."

The Prime Minister, sad and shaken, went up on deck and stood there, gazing into the sky. Upon the chill and vacant twilight blazed Halley's Comet—which, visiting the European heavens but once in a century, had arrived with appalling promptness to blaze forth the death of a king.

In London, darkness was gradually relinguishing the bleak façade of the dead king's palace and the crowds which still surrounded it, like the rising of a curtain upon some expensive melodrama, where the electric dawn gradually reveals a scene thronged with mourners. But here Mr. Asquith held the stage alone, the only visible human being within the ghostly margins of sea and sky, staring up at that punctual omen. A character from one of Voltaire's tragedies would have done justice to this magian situation with an *où suis-je?* or *Juste Ciel!*; but neither Mr. Asquith's temperament nor his rather stolid figure had any business to monopolize so pregnant a scene.

He has recorded it in one lightless sentence in his *Fifty Years of British Parliament*, and one can imagine his face, faintly illuminated in the twilight, a bland and weary face, in which frankness and reserve had long fought themselves to a stand-still. A touch of flamboyance in the long white hair, a hint of fantasy at the corners of the mouth gave this face a certain incongruity, as though a passage of correct and scholarly prose had been set up in too fanciful a type. Mr. Asquith was essentially a prosaic character.

The historian of pre-war England is at

From George Dangerfield, *The Strange Death of Liberal England* (New York, 1935). Reprinted by permission of Harrison Smith & Robert Hass, pp. 3–5, 7–16, 18–21, 24–27, 30–31, 71–72, 74–81, 95–96, 137–145, 147–150, 215–217, 230–235.

one grave disadvantage. Upon the face of every character he deals with there has stiffened a mask of facts, which only the acid of time can dissolve. Two centuries from now, Mr. Asquith will be a fiction, a contrivance of taste, sensibility, and scholarship; perhaps they will see him then as a man extravagantly moderate, who was facing at this precise moment four of the most immoderate years in English history.

Such is the brief opening scene of a political tragi-comedy. And since dramatic irony consists of the audience's knowing what the actor does not know, it is at least an ironical scene. History unfortunately has decreed that the rest of the play should be somewhat wanting in nobility and balance; that it should be hysterical, violent, and inconclusive: a mere fragment of a play, with the last act unwritten. Yet, before the curtain was hastily called down in August, 1914, Mr. Asquith and the Liberal Party of which he was such a placid leader had already been dealt a mortal wound; and this he had no means of telling, as he stood on the damp deck, thinking kindly of the late king.

* * *

The England upon which Mr. Asquith landed in May, 1910, was in a very peculiar condition. It was about to shrug from its shoulders—at first irritably, then with violence—a venerable burden, a kind of sack. It was about to get rid of its Liberalism.

Liberalism in its Victorian plenitude had been an easy burden to bear, for it contained—and who could doubt it?—a various and valuable collection of gold, stocks, bibles, progressive thoughts, and decent inhibitions. It was solid and sensible and just a little mysterious; and though one could not exactly *gambol* with such a weight on one's shoulders, it permitted one to walk in a dignified manner and even to execute from time to time those eccentric little steps which are so necessary to the health of Englishmen.

Whatever his political convictions may have been, the Englishman of the '70s and '80s was something of a liberal at heart. He believed in freedom, free trade, progress, and the Seventh Commandment. He also believed in reform. He was strongly in favor of peace—that is to say, he liked his wars to be fought at a distance and, if possible, in the name of God. In fact, he bore his Liberalism with that air of respectable and passionate idiosyncrasy which is said to be typical of his nation, and was certainly typical of Mr. Gladstone and the novels of Charles Dickens.

But somehow or other, as the century turned, the burden of Liberalism grew more and more irksome; it began to give out a dismal, rattling sound; it was just as if some unfortunate miracle had been performed upon its contents, turning them into nothing more than bits of old iron, fragments of intimate crockery, and other relics of a domestic past. What *could* the matter be? Liberalism was still embodied in a large political party; it enjoyed the support of philosophy and religion; it was intelligible, it was intelligent, and it was English. But it was also slow; and it so far transcended politics and economics as to impose itself upon behavior as well. For a nation which wanted to revive a sluggish blood by running very fast and in any direction, Liberalism was clearly an inconvenient burden.

As for the Liberal Party, it was in the unfortunate position of having to run, too. It was the child of Progress, which is not only an illusion, but an athletic illusion, and which insists that it is better to hurl oneself backwards than to stand still. By 1910, the Liberals had reached a point where they could no longer advance; before them stood a barrier of Capital which they dared not attack. Behind them stood the House of Lords.

In its political aspect, the House of Lords was extremely conservative, quite stupid, immensely powerful, and a determined enemy of the Liberal Party. It was also an essential enemy. If anything went wrong, if one's radical supporters became too insistent, if one's inability to advance became too noticeable, one could always blame the Lords. It was therefore a melancholy fate which decreed that the Liberals should turn upon their hereditary foe; that they should spend their last energies on beating it to its knees; and should thereupon themselves—expire.

It was this impending and paradoxical crisis—this battle between the Liberals and the Lords—which had assisted Edward VII into his grave, and which now confronted a new and not very popular king called George V.

* * *

In 1903, when Joseph Chamberlain—who had proved how insubstantial were party differences by being a Unitarian, a radical and a Conservative at one and the same time—returned from South Africa with a plea for protective tariffs, it was unfortunate that his voice should have sounded like the voice of Cassandra, that unwelcome prophetess. But so it was. The Conservatives were drifting out of popularity like a swimmer caught in the undertow. Their prestige had suffered as the Boer War dragged on and England discovered how much blood it cost to run an Empire, particularly when that blood was spent in the prolonged and frequently ludicrous pursuit of a number of undaunted Dutch farmers. The Imperialist cause was useful enough so long as it kept the country in a state of sentimental rage; it had even divided the Liberals into two warring factions, slow to forgive each other: but now something realistic had to be done if the Empire were not to dwindle back into what a Liberal statesman had once described as "one of the most idle and ill-contrived systems that ever disgraced a nation."

So Chamberlain decided to prove, with characteristic force, that the Empire was a paying proposition. Markets had begun it, by markets it should live. The scheme he had in mind was this: to build a tariff wall around England for the single purpose of knocking holes in it, through which Imperial goods might pass; for you could not ask favors of the colonies without having something to give in return, and the colonies, alas, were all protectionist. The proposal was an ingenious one; yet the mere description of this singular Empire, free trader at heart and protectionist in all its limbs, was enough to damn the describer. For it carried with it one implication which nobody cared to face in 1903; it meant that England was no longer commercial dictator of the world; that the Empire of Free Trade must soon become one with Nineveh and Tyre.

Chamberlain had to show how true this was, but his words were heresy and defeatism to all but the very few. Free Trade had been an article of British faith—whether Liberal or Conservative—since the repeal of the Corn Laws: it had been a faith to which America and Europe had subscribed because they were in no position to do anything else; it had been rooted in the backwardness of other countries. To Englishmen of the nineteenth century it had represented that combination of the ideal and the profitable which is peculiarly English—while it stilled their consciences, it stuffed their pockets. From time to time the cry of Protection had been raised, but always in lean years and wavering accents.

Chamberlain wrecked his party. The 1906 elections, fought around this prophetic, precarious, and unpopular issue, resulted in a Liberal landslide.

But the Liberal Party which came back to Westminster with an overwhelming majority was already doomed. It was like an army protected at all points except for one vital position on its flank. With the election of fifty-three Labor representatives, the death of Liberalism was pronounced; it was no longer the Left. The Conservatives might have consoled themselves with the fact that they represented a logical Right; they might have waited to see what would come. But theirs was the gift of tongues, not of divination. To them, as to their opponents and the country at large, this Labor contingent rapidly lost its terror. Even its twenty-nine professed socialists, those scandalous and impertinent revolutionaries, seemed prepared to vote with the Liberal majority, to wear frock coats, to attend royal garden parties, to become as time passed just a minor and far from militant act in the pantomime of Westminster.

The Conservatives were as sad and quarrelsome a pack as ever bayed a Liberal moon. And it was now, in this desolate political midnight to which Chamberlain had condemned them, that they turned to an old and faithful ally, an ally with whose aid—they openly but not wisely declared—they could run the country in or out of power. They turned to the House of Lords.

The House of Lords had been forgotten for nearly twelve years.

* * *

In '84 and '94 the Liberals had threatened this hereditary obstacle with a large curbing of its powers, though nobody seemed to take these threats with quite the seriousness they deserved. A Commons sufficiently goaded could turn the House of Lords into a harmless jest by persuading the Crown to create such a horde of new noblemen as would overwhelm, with an obedient Liberal vote, any Conservative opposition their lordships could bring against them. And it was precisely this remote and laughable contingency which, in 1906, Mr. Balfour and his Conservative minority refused to consider. And, refusing, ran themselves into one of the strangest constitutional comedies in English history.

It was clearly unwise to vex an opponent who had just been returned to Parliament with one of those majorities which mean that the people have spoken—to vex him, that is, otherwise than with words. The wise course would have been to wait. No government, however strongly supported in the Commons, can resist the melancholy climate of popular opinion, the gradual erosions of disillusion and boredom. The Liberal majority, as afterwards appeared, was built of showy but not very durable stuff; its splendid and somewhat arrogant 1906 façade would very soon have flaked and stained.

* * *

The Conservatives' tactics were simple, childlike, and brutal. In the Commons, they could only irritate their opponents with words: they looked to the obedient House of Lords to do the heavy work. And the Lords began by mutilating Mr. Augustine Birrell's Education Bill beyond hope of repair. Education in those days was a mysterious labyrinth, down whose crooked paths the Church of England and its sectarian opponents endlessly chased one another, fighting over what kind of religious teaching should be handed out to the children of England's poor. This being a Liberal bill, the Church of England naturally got the worst of it; for the Church was traditionally Conservative. But when the Lords killed it, nobody except the more rigid Nonconformists wept a tear over its perplexed and barren corpse, although Mr. Lloyd George—who pillaged the Scriptures without pity to adorn his speeches—immediately pronounced against the evil of hereditary rule.

In the same session their lordships rejected a Plural Voting Bill, designed to correct that old-fashioned injustice whereby certain property holders could vote in more than one place. This was a frankly party measure, and the Liberals contented themselves with threatening, through the mouth of their Prime Minister, Sir Henry Campbell-Bannerman, that "the resources of the Commons are not exhausted." Meanwhile and with merely the politest whisper of a grumble the Lords passed a Trade Disputes Bill which, backed by Labor and intended to soothe the justly enraged Trade Unions, was altogether too dangerous to tamper with.

(It was when legislation of this sort appeared that the two political parties at Westminster underwent a sorry transfiguration, becoming one body with two vexatious heads. Each party, with a delicately unconvincing air of being elsewhere, was treading a crude path of socialism: under twentieth century conditions, with a partly enfranchised and largely dissatisfied working class, they could not do otherwise. The Conservatives, who looked back to the subtle radicalism of Disraeli and the more distant paternal schemes of Peel and St. John, followed this path with less concern than their opponents. The Liberals still cherished at heart the teachings of Cobden and Bright, believed that state intervention was unforgivable, and watched with a growing apprehension the abyss which was opening between their theory and their practice. That abyss was eventually to swallow them up. Meanwhile, as a kind of capitalist left wing, they advanced upon social reform with noisy mouths and mouselike feet.)

Their lordships next slaughtered a Licensing Bill, the object of which was to curtail the number of public houses. In any Protestant country liquor, religion, and politics are likely to go hand in hand. In England, the Conservatives and the Established Church (whose priesthood was and is a gentleman's profession) traditionally believed in a man's right to drink strong waters: the Liberals and the Chapel (that is to say, the Wesleyans, Congregationalists, Unitarians, and other severe, independent and socially vulgar sects) were inclined to protest, and sometimes even to believe, that drink was the Devil. In the public houses, therefore, the Conservatives had a nice little chain of political fortresses, where their cause was loyally upheld by poor men in their cups; and these were not to be surrendered at any cost.

The country as a whole would have supported the House of Lords in this latest move, if their lordships had not set about it in a highly unprincipled manner. Instead of waiting to slay the bill with the courteous slow poison of a day's debate, two hundred and fifty noblemen (apparently encouraged by a Conservative victory in a Peckham by-election) met in open conclave at Lansdowne House, and there, in Lord Lansdowne's drawing room, voted its death. This was to insult not merely the Liberal party, not merely the Temperance enthusiast, but every right-thinking man in the country. When the Bill appeared in the House of Lords, it was already dead, "slain by the stiletto in Berkeley Square," and not worth debating. And Mr. Balfour still smiled upon these tactics, affable and unconcerned: through the Upper Chamber he was running the country, for all his pitiful minority in the House of Commons.

* * *

To Number Eleven, Downing Street, traditionally the Home of the Chancellor of the Exchequer, Mr. David Lloyd George had now moved his goods and chattels. He had left his former office of President of the Board of Trade to Mr. Winston Churchill, that volatile young convert from Conservatism, who complained bitterly that Mr. Lloyd George had taken all the plums, and who originated unemployment insurance.

Mr. George was a man set apart from his other colleagues on the Asquith cabinet. For one thing he had an irresponsible sense of humor; for another, he represented—or seemed to represent—all those dangerous and possibly subversive opinions which Liberalism, in its grave game of progress, was forced to tolerate. He was a great vote-catcher. His whole career had been set in terms of drama—to be correct, of sentimental drama: he had played his part with inspired and frequently sincere abandon; and his audience had spattered him generously with roses and eggs, both of which he seemed to enjoy.

If his convictions had been otherwise than emotional, he would have been a Socialist by this time. When he first exploded into English politics, an angry little solicitor from an uncouth, starved district in Wales, he brought with him something alien and dangerous. He was less a Liberal than a Welshman on the loose. He wanted the poor to inherit the earth, particularly if it was the earth of rich English landlords; and he wanted this with a sly, semi-educated passion which struck his parliamentary colleagues as being in very bad form.

The Boer War first brought him into prominence. He fought against it tooth and nail, and became generally hated as a leading pro-Boer—until the sad and sanguinary farce was over, when he was suddenly recognized as a man of vision.

But it may have been this successful termination to what had been, after all, a genuine campaign—a campaign inspired by deep personal distrust of empires and all imperial butchery—which turned his thoughts from the problems of maintaining a one-man Welsh revolution to the remote and dazzling chances of becoming an English prime minister. From then onwards he identified himself more closely with political Liberalism, putting himself before his party and his party before his principles. He became the idol of the radicals. Gentlemen of conservative tendencies and little humor (among whom, one cannot help feeling, were numbered in spirit most of his political colleagues) used to grumble that he would make a poor companion on a tiger hunt. And he would. He would have been on the tiger's side.

Fate, rather than Mr. Asquith, seemed to have promoted him to the Exchequer. In composing his 1909 Budget he was faced with an enormous deficit, and forced to create new revenue for the Army, the Navy and Old Age Pensions. This was exactly the sort of position he was happiest in; he decided that now, when the financial outlook was particularly dark, was the time to attack.

The Budget he then contrived came to be known as the "People's Budget," because it aimed a rude blow at the rich, and more especially at the Lords. It attacked the one interest which the Lords were known to cherish—the Land, the close and fruitful Goshen of society. Mr. Lloyd George proposed an increase in death duties, a duty on undeveloped land—the present value of which, he declared, was a brazen fiction—a duty on coal and mineral royalties, and a reversion duty on the termination of leases: to these he added, by way of revenge for the Lansdowne house "stiletto party," tremendous duties on the liquor trade; and, as an appeal to socialist opinion, a super-tax on all incomes over £5,000 a year.

According to Mr. John Burns, ex-Labor leader and Liberal careerist, the Cabinet deliberated upon this alarming document "like nineteen rag-pickers round a 'eap of muck." Most of them could probably see that in practice it was largely unworkable. Some of them were allied by birth, and all by friendship, with the rich whom it assaulted. And yet it had three advantages which could not be overlooked. It invested the whole party with an aura of progress which was badly needed after three none too progressive years in office; it was a loud champion of Free Trade; and it was a wonderful trap to catch the House of Lords in. To humble the House of Lords was the devout, vindictive wish of all good Liberals.

The question now was—how silly would their lordships be? By constitutional tradition, they could veto everything but a Budget: yet here was a Budget crying to be vetoed. It was like a kid, which sportsmen tie up to a tree in order to persuade a tiger to its death; and at its loud, rude bleating the House of Lords began to growl.

Their lordships prowled around it in their minds, meditating the last fatal leap. Should they kill it or not? If they vetoed it, the Government would have to resign, and Mr. Asquith would go to the country not merely on the question of whether this Free Trade Budget was a good thing or not but also on the question of whether their lordships' power of veto was a good thing or not. And if the Liberals were reëlected, with however slender a majority, then the House of Lords would be in for trouble—a very fantastic kind of trouble, involving the not altogether credible creation of several hundred brand new Liberal peers.

Mr. Balfour in the Commons, and the Marquess of Lansdowne in the Lords, were all for letting the Budget pass. But the House of Lords had grown reckless, and its large Conservative majority of obscure and far from intelligent peers was in no mood to take advice.

* * *

By a vote of 300 to 75, the Budget was rejected, constitutional precedent defied, the die cast.

Next morning, Mr. Asquith announced that the rights of the Commons had been rudely challenged, and that he had no choice but to advise an immediate dissolution. Vainly Mr. Balfour argued that the Budget was less a Money Bill than a new and brigandly fiscal policy: it was too late to save the day. In triumph, the Liberal cabinet resigned.

After a month of very dull electioneering, the country went to the polls in small numbers and recorded a lethargic opinion. As a result, the Liberals were so reduced, and the Conservatives so swollen, as to be almost equal in numbers: the Irish and Labor Parties held the balance of power.

Small wonder if, looking over these dispiriting figures, Liberals began to wonder whether they had not fallen into their own pit. If their party was to stay in power, it could only do so with Irish help. Betrayed Parnell's dream had come true at last. The Act of Union between England and Ireland, so disreputable in its origins, so lamentable in its history, had at last revealed its great constitutional weakness. It had bestowed the control of Parliament upon a handful of men to whom England was an enemy, and whose support could only be won at the stiff price of Irish Home Rule. By these elections of January, 1910, the Act of Union killed itself.

Killing itself, it killed the Liberal party: thereafter Mr. Asquith and his colleagues were never to be separated from their Irish allies, for whom in their hearts they had no use at all. Irish Home Rule had been buried with Gladstone; in 1910, it was an academic question, no Englishman cared for it. And yet, if this "People's Budget," having survived an election, were to pass through the Commons once again, Mr. Asquith needed Irish votes. And the Irish were seriously opposed to Mr. Lloyd George's land and liquor taxes; and would only join in passing them, and in the subsequent assault upon the House of Lords, on the strict understanding that Home Rule would follow.

Moreover they, and certain more radical members of the Liberal party, demanded that, before the Budget was passed and England saved from a threatening financial chaos, definite steps should be taken towards limiting the Lords' powers of veto. The mild majority of Mr. Asquith's following and all the Opposition called for the Budget to be taken first. On February 21, speaking with unusual nervousness, Mr. Asquith declared that the Budget should go up to the Lords at once; faced a radical mutiny for the next week; meditated resignation; and eight days later announced in the House that his program was "somewhat modified." He now proposed merely such financial measures as would tide the Government over the next few weeks; these passed, he would offer certain resolutions concerning their lordships' veto. The meaning of this was clear to everybody. Faced with an Irish and Radical desertion, he had thrown away all but the simplest pretense of independent action: in order to keep himself in power, he had made a bargain with the Irish. Under the gentle mockery of Mr. Balfour, English constitutional history took on a new and forbidding shape—how forbidding, indeed how disastrous, time was yet to show.

But neither the Liberals nor their tyrannical Irish allies could have their way with the House of Lords, without the help of one life, now very near its finish. The

Government's next step was to pass a Bill through the Commons, limiting the Lords' veto; it would then be sent up to the Lords, who would scarcely pass it and vote their own death, unless they were bullied into doing so. And the only man who could bully them was Edward VII.

Edward VII faced this contingency with a justifiable uneasiness. Should the Lords refuse to destroy themselves, he would be advised to exercise his royal prerogative and create a multitude of new Liberal peers, who would obediently vote whichever way the Government told them. It was in his choice to exercise or not to exercise this prerogative. But it was generally supposed that his promise to exercise it would be enough; under such a threat, their lordships would have to yield. Better to vote their death themselves, than to have it voted for them; better to die as they were, a decent corpse, than to die ludicrously swollen with Liberal peerages. So everybody thought, and so King Edward thought, when he promised not to stand in Mr. Asquith's way. But he would not, he said, absolutely guarantee to use his prerogative unless there were another election: if the country did not change its mind, if the Liberals were again returned, even to such power as they now held, he would do whatever he was advised to do.

Disgusted as the prospect of being used against the Lords, with whom he rather naturally sympathized, he did suggest a compromise. Of the six hundred peers, he proposed, let one hundred only have the right to vote, and let this one hundred be divided equally between Liberals and Conservatives. He made this suggestion hopefully to the Marquesses of Crewe and Lansdowne, respectively leaders of the Liberal and Conservative parties in the Lords; but neither nobleman could agree. What sort of selection would be made, they asked, but of the most obdurate and irreconcilable within either party? At that, the King determined that the choice no longer rested with him; he must do whatever the Government wanted. "Thank God," he said to Mr. Reginald McKenna, the First Lord of the Admiralty, "it's not my business."

*   *   *

The whole importance of this quarrel, which the Lloyd George Budget finally precipitated, lies in its reference to two very simple propositions: aristocracy must be powerful; aristocracy must be responsible. English aristocracy, more ancient in principle than in birth, had fought for, and won; and was now losing its economic power: it was the mournful duty of politics to shadow forth its loss of responsibility by taking away its parliamentary leadership.

It would be easy to relegate this dispute to a mere phase in party warfare, and to forget its large implications. But this was no parochial affair. It was a struggle between two doomed powers: between the middle-class philosophy which was Liberalism and the landed wealth which passed for aristocracy and found its living symbol in the House of Lords. With the Lords' power of veto went all those claims to economic leadership which had formerly belonged to the owners of great estates.

And if Mr. Asquith's Resolutions and his Parliament Bill meant anything, they meant that the land's political power was on the wane as well. Away with it, and away with English aristocracy, too: it had become too old-fashioned to do its work.

There is a barbarism in politics, not unhealthy, which decrees the death of any institution which has lost its economic meaning; just as savage kings and chieftains were once slaughtered when they were no longer able to lead in battle or beget children. (But those who made themselves the instruments of this archaic doom had to be young and healthy and brave. Otherwise the same doom would come upon them.

Could the Liberal party succeed where the House of Lords had failed? Could it govern the country? Or was it perhaps too feeble and too faint-hearted to avoid, in its turn, a swift and correct destruction?)

*   *   *

The consequences of the Parliament Act were not heroic. Biographers of those gentlemen who were fated to play a leading rôle in the domestic events of the next three years have treated this period in the lives of their heroes with a certain nonchalance: they have, in fact, hurried past it; and have taken up the thread of their story at the point where England's statesmen were to be seen in a more advantageous light—directing, muddling, or dying in the most hideous war in human history. English biography adroitly stops in 1910 and starts again in 1914. But the story of these years deserves to be told, if only for the spectacle it affords us of a democracy passing from introspection to what looks very like nervous breakdown. Unfortunately it cannot be told with the biographer's privilege of selecting only what pleases him; the procession of minor incidents must be allowed to shuffle its way through these pages unhindered by any nice considerations of art or form.

I set it in motion with something of an apology. One day in the life of a contemporary dictator will provide more instances of fruitless insanity, of misplaced tyranny and sudden caprice than will appear in all these pages put together. This is not a record of personalities but of events; and not of great events but of little ones, which, working with the pointless industry of termites, slowly undermined England's parliamentary structure until, but for the providential intervention of a world war, it would certainly have collapsed. The structure remains, a not unsightly patchwork: it is still agreeably haunted by one of its former inhabitants, who slowly died there during the years 1910–1914. It was in these years that that highly moral, that generous, that dyspeptic, that utterly indefinable organism known as the Liberal Party died the death. It died from poison administered by its Conservative foes, and from disillusion over the inefficacy of the word "Reform." And the last breath which fluttered in this historical flesh was extinguished by War.

*   *   *

With the House of Lords no longer able to prevent it, Home Rule was now a certainty. Mr. Asquith had promised it, when he bargained for Irish support for his Budget and his Parliament Bill. Nobody knows exactly what bargain he had struck then, whether it was a written pledge or just a gentleman's agreement; he and John Redmond, the Irish leader, carried that secret with them to their graves.

It may have been merely a gentleman's agreement, for Redmond was always to preserve a rather touching faith in the Liberal Party. He succeeded Parnell, when memories of that tragic O'Shea divorce case still offended the delicate nostrils of English Protestantism; and, just as he himself was never hurt by scandal, so was he never touched by that cold flame which burned in his former leader. He was fond of Parliament; its dignified ritual, its devices, and subterfuges, and intrigues all meant more to him than perhaps they should mean to an Irish leader, and it was often said of him that he had been so long in Westminster that he had forgotten what Ireland was like. In appearance he resembled a hawk: not, indeed, the hawk whose poised shadow casts a silence on the hedgerows beneath him, not the "blue bleak ember"; but a tamed and weary hawk. And it was not Parliament alone which had tamed him: beneath his outside of remote and almost Roman gravity there beat the heart of a squire. And whenever in the next few years occasion arose for his outside to prove itself, to present a stern and implacable opposition to Liberal compromise, to insist on full payment for his earlier support— then that betraying heart, the heart of a gentleman with a nice little estate in County Wicklow, would suddenly get the better of him. He would think, he would retreat, he would half yield: and then the occasion had passed. He was a living contradiction; and it was the fate of the Liberal Party to give itself into the hands of a contradiction and not of a Parnell. A Parnell would probably have been driven to put it out of office; a contradiction could only lead it deeper and deeper into the mires, and the mists, and the squalls of Irish politics—and eventually lose it there.

What Asquith and Redmond had agreed upon would have been simplicity itself under one condition—a united nationalist Ireland. To separate Ireland from its Union with England, *that* would not have been the major operation which Gladstone had attempted: not in 1911. In 1911 Ireland was surprisingly respectable, and the old picture of its lean, outrageous peasantry, its filthy cabins which bred starvation and treachery, its unsuitable religion, its illogical refusal to see the beauties of lowliness and reverence as ordained by the Anglican Catechism, its permanent lust for stabbing England in the back—this old picture, so lamentably ill-conceived because conceived by an oppressor, was already fading from the English mind.

* * *

But Ireland was not united. In the northern province of Ulster there lived a community of Protestants, descended sometimes from dour Presbyterian Lowland Scots, sometimes from English settlers. Ireland which, with the colored breath of its climate and the odor of its haunted soil, had tamed the Norman and the Dane, and absorbed the Belgians in Wexford, and seen even the remains of Cromwell's soldiers yield before the gentle charm of Tipperary — Ireland had laid its hand upon even the most forbidding foreign elements in Ulster. A surprisingly large number of original Celts survived the infamous "clearances" and remained, in unregenerate Catholicism, to fill the southern counties of Ulster and sometimes to mingle the unhappy charm of their blood with the cold blood to the north of them: the mists and the rains and the long twilights worked their spell. And the result had been not to soften the Ulster Protestant but to set him apart. The Ulster Protestant liked nobody but himself.

He was the Orangeman. Every year, on the anniversary of the Battle of the Boyne when William of Orange slaughtered the bewildered and abandoned forces of James II—("Change kings," they shouted, "and we'll fight you again")—he beat his knuckles raw on the drum. Those monotonous Orange drums were the voice of Ulster. They beat out a contempt for all Catholics; they were the savage undertone of that Protestant Ascendancy which had once driven the best Catholic families to live in underground cellars, which had persecuted and impoverished and fattened on Southern Ireland, and which still remained—in the shape of a disestablished but unfortunately not dispossessed Church —to fill the ancient cathedrals and churches with the mingled smell of rotting hassocks and inefficient scrubbing. The Protestant Ascendancy, though essentially it had been a profitable union of landlords and clergymen, had always smiled upon the northern Orangeman; he was part of it in the sense that he had been spared by it, and he was part of it in the sense that he had learned from it. He utterly despised his Catholic neighbors, they were no countrymen of his: they were a lower order of human being. "The crown of the causeway," ran one of his typical rhymes, "on road or street, and the Papishes under my feet." Another name for the Catholics was "Croppies." Mr. Wingfield-Stratford quotes a passage from one characteristic Orange toast to the memory of William III, the victor of the Boyne: "And may all Croppies be rammed, slammed, jammed and damned into the great gun that is in Athlone, and may I be standing by with a lighted torch to blow them in innumerable fragments over the Hill of Blastation. . . ." The Orange population of Ulster was thrifty and industrious but not lovable.

And it had no love for England. It was quite alone; it owed no allegiance to anyone but itself and the grim God it had fashioned in its own likeness. England was a convenience, England existed to see that no Catholic Irish Parliament ever controlled affairs in Ulster; and at all times when such control seemed unlikely, the Ulsterman was a convinced and stubborn radical who, at the least sign of interference from England, turned angry and rebellious.

By some trick of history which only Southern Irishmen could understand, who still thought of Ulster as the fighting province, the "right arm of Ireland"—from Ulster came some of the greatest of Irish patriots. And yet it was this inexplicable province, whose sons could rise to the heights of selfless patriotism and sink to the sourest depths of bigotry, which alone stood between Ireland and Home Rule.

Ulster's support of the Union with England was partly religious and partly economic. To its fears of Catholic intolerance, of priestly despotism, was added the premonition that, under an Irish parliament, Catholics would take all the best positions, and once in possession of them, would have no ability to perform what they had undertaken. Belfast merchants and manufacturers were convinced that an Irish parliament would ruin them, through taxation, through mismanagement, through legislation which would favor agriculture at the expense of industry. After all, they argued, the Catholics of Ireland had for generations been deprived of administrative experience. What did Southern Ireland know about industry? When one tried to answer that question it became all too clear that England had first of all reduced the Catholic Irish, through starvation and exile, to a point where they were properly "available" for industry, and had then seen to it that industry was never available for them. When Grattan's Parliament ended in that corrupt Union with England, all hopes of an industrial Ireland ended with it, and while other nations passed on into the nineteenth century Ireland lingered in the eighteenth. Spiritually and economically, southern Ireland was still in the eighteenth

century when Asquith and Redmond struck their bargain.

It is not to be supposed that English Conservatives had any feelings of bosom friendship for Ulster. Ulster's "loyalty" was loyalty to Ulster; and nobody could quite forget that when the Board of National Education was first set up, Ulster had blossomed overnight with revolutionary "gunclubs," and that when the Church Act was passed Ulster had threatened to "kick the Queen's Crown into the Boyne." That was not so very long back; and in 1911 all its talk of British citizenship, and Crown, and Empire, and Constitution was simply a way of finding synonyms for the Protestant Ascendancy. No, Ulster was not lovable, and the Conservative Party did not love it; but, looking round for a weapon with which to replace the Lords' veto, its eye lit upon . . . Ulster's bigotry. With Ulster's bigotry it could break the Liberal Party.

What a lovely argument lay in its mouth! The Liberals were professed lovers of freedom, yet here they were, all ready to offer Ireland Home Rule at the expense of the Ulster minority; they were offering something which might perhaps only be achieved by the forcible coercion of the northern Protestants; they had impaled themselves on the horns of a dilemma and, with the proper political pressure, they might easily perform there a really very humorous act of self-immolation. Deprived of the Lords' veto, the Conservatives turned from Westminster, and, with a cynical abandon, started to beat the Orange drum.

The Tory Party, in the course of absorbing the doubtful or angry Liberal, had acquired another *alias*—it was also the Unionist Party. *Unionists* were originally gentlemen who could not see eye to eye with Mr. Gladstone in the matter of Home Rule for Ireland—in other words, the Conservatives plus Mr. Joseph Chamberlain and his ex-Liberal following; then they became gentlemen who believed in solving the Boer problem *vi et armis*; then they were the advocates of militant imperialism: and now, when the question of Home

Rule was once more in the air, their very name implied that they were ready to resist Home Rule by any means that came to hand. From Joseph Chamberlain they had inherited something rather less reasonable than Tariff Reform; they had inherited a taste for fighting, simply for fighting's sake.

In the days of Mr. Gladstone, Home Rule had been something to fight against, because Imperialism had not then been tarnished with Boer blood. Home Rule, to the imperialist of the '90s, was like gashing the very heart of a glorious Empire. But the imperialist of 1911 was not quite so romantically minded; he knew perfectly well that to give Ireland a Parliament, which, at its best, could be little better than a glorified County Council, would do the Empire no harm at all; and he had more than a suspicion that an unsupported Ulster could probably be made to consent without too much difficulty. The word "Unionist" fitted snugly round the Conservative mood, like an iron glove around a fist. It had very little to do with Ireland: it had a great deal to do with beating the Liberal Party into an irremediable mess of political blood and brains.

And the Unionists had acquired a new leader. In November, 1911, Mr. Balfour resigned from that position, explaining in a characteristic speech to his constituents of the City of London that he was too tired. He was succeeded by Andrew Bonar Law. Bonar Law was chosen by a compromise, since the party could not decide between the equally powerful claims of Messrs. Walter Long and Austen Chamberlain; but, like many men who are chosen through compromise, he was exactly suited to the particularly brutal policy the Unionists were about to adopt.

He was a man *without unction*—so Sir Walter Raleigh had described him in one of his letters, adding unreasonably that he loved men without unction. If so, Sir Walter was one of the few people in England who could have felt anything much more than a liking for Andrew Bonar Law, who contrived to hide a mild and retiring disposition behind an appearance of rasping, uncomfortable self-consciousness. He was a Scotch-Canadian, and a Presbyterian; his father had once occupied an Ulster manse. His face was sad, his forehead crumpled; he had an unfortunate habit of saying the wrong thing in debate. He was absolutely honest, and he was excessively Tory in the matter of having no political imagination whatsoever: when attacked by men more subtle in dialectics than himself, he generally took refuge in a remarkably unpleasing rudeness.

The really dangerous thing about Andrew Bonar Law was the fact that he was too close in spirit to Ulster's bigotry: his leadership provided an admirable screen for the cynical manoeuvres of his colleagues on the Opposition Bench.

* * *

The Tories have been kindly treated by history, which has overshadowed their Ulster conspiracy with the vast bulk of the subsequent War, so that today this conspiracy is almost forgotten; and they have been kindly treated by psychology, which contends, not without truth, that England was in such a dangerous state of hysteria in the last two years of 1912–1914, that even the most outrageous acts then committed must find some excuse. But the Tory mind, none the less, did concoct nothing less than a rebellion in those years; and perhaps the most disagreeable thing about this rebellion was that it was set on foot in the name of Loyalty.

Since it ended with nothing more sanguinary than the hasty slaughter of some few Irish citizens in Bachelor's Walk in Dublin, it might be considered of very small importance: but in its peculiar way it is one of the most monstrous events in English constitutional history, and certainly the most deadly event in the history of English Liberalism; for in that obscene little spatter of blood on the Dublin quays the word *Finis* was written to the great Liberal battles of the nineteenth century. . . .

The Tory philosophy, up to the beginning of the War, might be summed up in this way: be Conservative about good things, and Radical about bad things. This philosophy, so far as can be seen, has only one flaw; it was always the Tories who decided what was good and what was bad. This kind of decision can be made time and time again with the best results; but it contains, in its very essence, some fatal and arbitrary elements, and the mere effort of having to make it has been known to produce any number of fanatics, tyrants, martyrs, minor prophets, and, indeed, most of the disagreeable creatures which have ever plagued this long-suffering planet. In 1912, the Tories decided that a Parliament controlled by a Liberal majority was a Bad thing.

Everything they did in the next two years was aimed, not against Home Rule, but against the very existence of Parliament. Because Liberalism was already almost moribund, in spite of its appearance of health, their conscious aim was to destroy Liberalism: because the whole mood of that pre-war England was sudden, somber, and violent, their unconscious desire was to ruin an institution which they were pledged to protect. An utterly constitutional party, they set out to wreck the Constitution; and they very nearly succeeded.

*   *   *

In Dublin on November 28, [1912] he [Bonar Law] made one of the most reckless speeches of his whole career:

"I remember this," he said, "that King James had behind him the letter of the law just as completely as Mr. Asquith has now. He made sure of it. He got the judges on his side by methods not dissimilar from those by which Mr. Asquith has a majority in the House of Commons on his side. There is another point to which I would specially refer. In order to carry out his despotic intention the King had the largest army which had ever been seen in England. What happened? There was no civil war. Why? Because his own army refused to fight for him."

A more extraordinary appeal to the Army had never been made, it is safe to say, by any Opposition leader. And when it was made, something died: that attitude of critical and grumbling respect for government, which had been fostered through over two hundred years of revolution and reform, expired upon Mr. Bonar Law's breath. It had to die: it was too old, and not healthy; but it was curious that a Tory leader should have pronounced its obsequies. The immediate effect of Mr. Bonar Law's speech became apparent as the year passed. The position of Parliament had shrunk — beneath this singular attack of politicians and generals—to something almost purely topographical. Parliament had become so many square yards in the Borough of Westminster; so many cubic feet of talkative air and pseudo-Gothic masonry; so many echoes in an inconvenient chamber where several hundred gentlemen sullenly debated. Its position in the English scene had been usurped by two forces—Sir Edward Carson[1] and, vague but menacing, the British Army.

*   *   *

If in the Tory Rebellion . . . there is something outrageous and desperate, something murderous even in its mildness, yet in the end the whole process seems to resolve itself into a political melodrama, moving with infinite slowness towards an unknown destination. The actors may rant as they please, the imitation thunders and lightnings roar and flicker, the backdrop with a parliament painted on it may be exchanged for a lurid suggestion of horror and despair —but still, when the echoes have faded and the lights are dimmed and the curtain goes down on that tedious and tawdry act, what have we left but the memory of some recognizable English politicians in the recognizable posture of having lost their heads?

But as the frock-coated cast goes through

[1] Edward Henry Carson, a prominent Conservative, Leader of the Ulster Unionist Council, 1911, and organiser of resistance to Home Rule. [EDITOR'S NOTE.]

its ill-directed paces, we are uncomfortably aware that we have missed something. The death of an attitude? An attitude of respect for the processes of democratic government? An attitude which in itself was no more than two hundred years old, and which was afterwards reborn—not with the same secure, complacent, and satisfying appearance—but reborn none the less?

There is more to it than that. In the menaces of Sir Edward Carson, . . . and the fulminations of Mr. Bonar Law, and the hesitations of Mr. Asquith, and even in the acquiescence of Mr. Balfour—was there not evident, horrible but inevitable word, a neurosis? To pursue a neurosis through the endless involutions of a political system; to observe, in the movements of those fundamentally decent figures, the effects of weariness, insecurity, and fear; to ask from what origin sprang those impulses which could make the legislators of England talk in terms of toy soldiers, and incredibly drag a party quarrel into the arena of civil war—such a task, from the very outset, seems quite impossible. Yet some such inquiry has to be made. For surely when an ancient Constitution is impiously investigated in a fit of bad temper, the historian is faced with a crisis which, in one shape or another, constantly recurs through the history of our times. The explanations are not difficult. The Land had lost its power, therefore the Lords lost theirs; the Irish, for the first time in the history of the Union, and with no Lords to defeat them, could impose their will on a weak Liberal cabinet; and the Liberal cabinet was weak because, in that stage of capitalism, it no longer represented an effective Left: no wonder the Tories tried, by such crude means as lay immediately at hand, to medicine this incurable economic sickness, and no wonder their methods seemed to hasten rather than delay its course. But are these really the explanations? Or rather, do they explain all that there is to explain? It is the habit of contemporary philosophy to mesh every succeeding crisis in the ordered and apparently inescapable nets of economic theory; but, somehow or other, when the

nets are dragged brimful into the light of day, one thing seems to have evaded them, and that the most important catch of all. They have been dropped into swarming waters at the likeliest times; they have been watched with skill and manœuvred with infinite patience; but they have never quite snared that inconvenient and unpredictable entity—the human soul. Yet it is the human soul which—as in all crises, so in the Tory Rebellion—finally disposes the course of events. To mention the word "soul" in connection with Sir Edward Carson, Mr. F. E. Smith, Mr. Bonar Law, Mr. Asquith, and Mr. Balfour might seem incongruous, not to say romantic, if by "soul" one meant that spiritual essence which variously manifests itself in the ecstasies of saints, the fugues of Bach, and the iambics of Aeschylus.

But—fortunately or unfortunately—the word is susceptible of a lower definition, and may even mean that irrational side of human nature which, for all the enlightenments of civilization still persists in responding to images so long buried in history that no one can positively say where they began or where they will end. This sort of irrational and unconscious element may possibly be discovered in the vagaries of pre-war English politicians; indeed, there is no avoiding it. For the Tory Rebellion was not merely a brutal attack upon an enfeebled opponent—that is to say, political; it was not merely the impassioned defense of impossible privileges—that is to say, economic; it was also, and more profoundly, the unconscious rejection of an established security. For nearly a century men had discovered in the cautious phrase, in the respectable gesture, in the considered display of reasonable emotions, a haven against those irrational storms which threatened to sweep through them. And gradually the haven lost its charms; worse still, it lost its peace. Its waters, no longer unruffled by the wind, ceased to reflect, with complacent ease, the settled skies, the untangled stars of accepted behavior and sensible conviction: and men, with a defiance they could not hope to understand, began to put forth upon little excursions into the vast, the dark, the driven seas beyond. When Mr. Bonar Law incited the army to mutiny, his boat was already out; when Sir Edward Carson played upon the fury of Orange Ulster, he had left the haven, too; and so with Mr. F. E. Smith, and Lord Halsbury, and Lord Hugh Cecil, and the rest. Would they manage to keep afloat, by bailing out with some little political bucket? Would they sink? Would they put back? These questions were never settled; for, alas, the waters in which they found themselves were soon to be adventured upon by the whole western world, to be widely strewn with the wreckage of liberal faiths, and to encompass us all today.

But the death of Liberal England—the various death of security and respectability —may not be considered simply as a loud prelude, passing suddenly into war. It was a brief but complete phase in the spiritual life of the nation. And though the Tory Rebellion refuses to reveal, in any kind of a satisfactory fashion, the irrational nature of this phase, the historian cannot excuse himself from seeking it elsewhere.

* * *

The politicians refuse to be anything but politicians; there remain the women. What can hardly be seen in the activities of one sex, may possibly discover itself—however reluctantly—in those of the other. On first thoughts, the activities of Englishwomen during those unnaturally distant years between 1910 and 1914 are merely an agreeable, disturbing extension of what had been going on for more than twenty years. *Emancipation* is the word; it conjures up all sorts of new visions—from tennis and bicycling to the inner sanctums of offices, where, for the first time, in all her glory, and at starvation wages, woman was beginning to compete with man. The most convenient way of approaching this question is through the wardrobe. The female form, as the century progressed towards war, was being released from the distortions and distentions of the Victorian era; no longer did woman insist, with what seems to our more modest gaze an extreme salaciousness, upon the erotic attractions of her hips and her buttocks, thrusting these portions of herself, well padded and beribboned, into the eye of the yearning male. By 1910 the womanly body had begun to look very like a womanly body. Corsets were reasonable, skirts scarcely dragged in the mire and the dust, evening gowns were more *svelte* than swollen. Towards 1912, daring ladies slashed their evening skirts well up to the knee, and set off their attractive slimness with outrageous head-dresses of plumes; and by day the influence of Bakst appeared in effective combinations of barbaric colors: and somehow the conversation whispered over luncheon tables and behind palms suited itself to these desirable changes.

The female wardrobe, with its endless combinations of colors and varieties of material, with its infinite suggestions of new social relationships, offers itself as a convenient short cut into history: but is the history thus arrived at by any chance true history? Is it in the peccadilloes of a "smart set," in the emancipated whisper in some fronded embrasure of a ducal drawing room, in the activities of a county tennis court, that the shadowy depths reveal themselves? The du Deffands and de Carrières of an earlier day, the Mrs. Asquiths of this Georgian world we are thinking of, are, it is true, an essential decoration, a guide-post even, a clew to mysteries long vanished: and yet, along with the wit, the wardrobe is faded. Where are they now, the silks and the feathers and the fans? How many men have tried to preserve, in the faint lisp of silk as it curtseys, in some exact description of an exotic perfume, in the nods and nuances of a salon, the very accents and distillations and subtleties of a buried past! And how few have succeeded! The light thus thrown shows up only what time itself has discarded as worthless.

. . . and in one place lay
Feathers and dust, today and yesterday.

But as we turn over the Georgian wardrobe there, among that reasonable collection of charming stuffs and shapes, appear two preposterous contrivances—a stiff starched collar, very like a man's, and a hard straw hat, very like a man's. And, as we contemplate these unappetizing, these almost incredible phenomena, we realize that the pre-war female wardrobe has, after all, led us straight into life. . . .

The early twentieth century woman would try at times, as accurately and uncomfortably as possible, to make herself look masculine. And when we ask, why did she try to make herself look masculine? —then, upon the heels of that apparently simple inquiry, there crowd such a host of warnings and suggestions, such a bevy of revolutionary causes from such unexplored depths, that we feel something like Odysseus, when he poured a little blood into a trench and discovered that he was faced with the whole assembly of hell. The stiff starched collar and the hard straw hat are, at best, inconsiderable clews, but they are positive; and it is a positive movement we are now to inquire into.

For the Women's Rebellion—the outrageous Suffragette Movement of 1910–1914 —was above all things a movement from darkness into light, and from death into life; and, like the Tory Rebellion, its unconscious motive was the rejection of a moribund, a respectable, a smothering security. The reasons for this are too manifold and too obscure to be pressed into a few paragraphs, but there is one which might profitably be selected for examination. Woman, through her new awareness of the possibilities of an abstract goal in life, was, in effect, suddenly aware of her longneglected masculinity. And the consequences of this were extreme. With a vital energy, the manifestations of which were abandoned and eccentric, she pursued her masculinity first into politics—which seemed the most likely thicket in which to bring it to bay—then into the secret recesses of her own being; and though her quarry was always agile enough to remain one

jump ahead of her, her pursuit was to be of incalculable service to the women who came after. At the time, to be sure, it did not seem so. The Suffragettes were always in a minority, and their behavior, to say the least of it, was neither sensible nor endearing. But if we follow them through all the steps of their peculiar career, we may get some notion of other forces then sweeping through England; until at last we may even catch a glimpse, fleeting but complete, of that new energy which rose like a phoenix from the strange death of the pre-war world and rushed headlong onto the battlefields of Flanders and the bloodstained beaches of Gallipoli.

Beneath the political and economic motives in the disintegration of Liberal England, there lies the psychological motive— the abandonment of security. In the case of the women it was the abandonment of what was, in the worst sense of the word, a *feminine* security.

The militant suffragettes did not actually become militant until November, 1910; and from then until the war they were always in the minority. This was only to be expected. For all her mistakes—and they were many and fantastic—the militant suffragette lived in the present, and must be enrolled among the makers of history. The process of making history can, in her case, be divided into two distinct stages. At first, her instinct warned her that only by asserting their masculinity could women hope to become women again, and for a time she was willing to make use of a long established argument and demand for women a political equality with men; in other words, she wanted the Vote. But it would be ingenuous to suppose that the suffragette was ultimately concerned with anything so reasonable as the suffrage. What good would the Vote do her, when and if she had it? The arguments in its favor were numerous and convincing, and she had them all at her finger tips: but did they go deep enough? Her instinct assured her that they did not. Gradually she began to draw upon the masculine element within herself, not simply as something which confirms an argument, but rather as a food which sustains and energizes life. And the food, reënforced by the repressions of a century, was not unnaturally too strong for her. Those high starched collars, those hard straw hats, what are they, after all, but the fugitive and casual symbols of acute psychological dyspepsia?

Beside the discomfort of her undigested masculinity (which made her increasingly arrogant towards men), the woman of the present—the pre-war suffragette—suffered from another and equally formidable affliction. She was haunted. Whether she sat or walked or talked or slept, in public and in private, there crept about her an enervating, a lax, a lamentable atmosphere —the cloudy desires of hundreds of thousands of unmarried women, condemned to do nothing. In this atmosphere of the unlived female life, which invaded—unasked and irresistible—the remotest rooms of her being, she was restless and irritable. Here too, it seemed, were to be discerned the scattered and wasting elements of a great female principle.

How were they to be fused once more? Her answer to this perplexing question was a revolutionary one—she must overthrow that personal security which had kept women lurking for so long behind the coat-tails of their men. . . .

This was the second stage in the making of pre-war feminine history. It was achieved in disorder, arrogance, and outrage. It was melodramatic, it was hysterical, it was in a hurry. . . .

* * *

Naturally enough, these Georgian suffragettes were odious to men, whom they regarded more and more as coarse and inferior creatures; but they were also odious to women. The majority of pre-war women lived in the past, clung to their respectable and moribund security, and dreaded even the limited independence which the Vote would assure them. And perhaps, in their heart of hearts, they knew that they were doomed—to live.

For the revolution was on its way, and the way it took was the way of all revolutions. Its end was a valuable one—the solidarity of women, the recovery of their proper place in the world; its means were violent and dubious. But no revolution has ever taken place without the sudden, the unbridled uprising of long suppressed classes and long ungratified desires; without cruelty and rage: nor is a revolution anything but the savage assault of the right instincts upon wrong ideals. The Georgian suffragette was not personally attractive, or noble, or *clairvoyante*. People who make history very seldom are. Providence has bestowed upon them an instinctive response to the unrecognized needs of the human soul, and though this response is often wry and more often ridiculous, life could scarcely progress without it. By 1910 the ideal of personal security through respectability had become putrid: therefore it was necessary that it should die. And to accomplish its death there assembled, crowding up from the depths of the female soul, as uncouth a collection of neglected instincts, hopes, hatreds, and desires, as thorough-going a psychological *jacquerie*, as ever came together at any time in human history.

* * *

The workers of England, united neither in their politics nor in their grievances, with no single desire for solidarity, yet contrived to project a movement which took a revolutionary course and might have reached a revolutionary conclusion; and how is this to be explained? The pre-war English worker was no *doctrinaire*. He could not be expected to respond to impressive theories and visionary speculations. He was consciously respectable, lawabiding, even reactionary. And yet from that world of his, into which legislation entered with such reluctance, and where nine-pence a week meant the difference between acute and normal discomfort, there rose such an assault upon Liberalism as put the two previous rebellions completely in the shade.

An assault upon Liberalism! If one dared approach a proletarian movement with an intuition instead of a theory, here would be the answer. For Liberalism, after all, implies rather more than a political creed or an economic philosophy; it is a profoundly conscience-stricken state of mind. It is the final expression of everything which is respectable, God-fearing, and frightened. The poor, it says, are always with us, and something must certainly be done for them: not too much, of course, that would never do; but something. The poor might reasonably be expected to have their own opinions about this; and, indeed, in certain periods of the Victorian era they gave vent to these opinions in a most disconcerting manner. But they, too, had been infected with the same disease.

"Several toasts were given" (so writes an observer of a workmen's dinner during the prolonged erection, in the '70s, of the Albert Memorial) "and many of the workmen spoke, almost all of them commencing by 'Thanking God that they enjoyed good health'; some alluded to the temperance that prevailed amongst them, others observed how little swearing was ever heard, whilst all said how pleased and proud they were to be engaged on so great a work." (v. *Queen Victoria* by Lytton Strachey, p. 324.)

Honest labor bears a lovely face. To do my duty in that state of life unto which it hath pleased God to call me. Was it against these complacent phrases, and all they meant, that the British workman finally revolted? Honest labor, the doing of duty, reverence towards one's betters—all these are the conditions of a certain kind of security; and these, too, have a fatal attraction for the independent mind. And what is Liberalism itself but something which preys upon the independent mind—Liberalism which proffers, at one moment, the necessary minimum of reform, and protests, at the next, that—such is the sanctity of contract—a workman has the right to sell his labor where he pleases and for any kind of wages that he can get? In the worst slums, the most underpaid districts of Victorian England, the doctrines of security and independence had twined their roots and grown large; and their seeds had been blown—by what unkindly winds!—into the less promising soil of the infant Trade Unions. The worker, too independent to believe that solidarity was his only hope, looked upon collective bargaining as almost a decent, almost one might say a humble, plea for better treatment. The contradiction could not be borne forever; a man cannot be simultaneously proud and prostrate: but on that contradiction was founded the respectability of the Victorian working classes.

Respectability . . . wasn't it *safe*, after all? How glibly could one maintain—with remarkable optimism, of course, but optimism is glib, too—that it guaranteed every man a living! Let a worker be honest, sober, God-fearing, industrious and—somehow or other, you could not say precisely how, but by some mysterious method of cautious interference—the State would see to it that he never went hungry. This was one of the chief articles in the Liberal creed, though it was unwritten and only whispered deep in the heart. And as the great Labor Unrest of 1910–1914 unfolds itself, might one not see it as a profoundly unconscious assault upon respectability, a vital revolution in the world of the soul?

Economics, to be sure, are extremely uneasy with a generalization such as this. And though the whole complexion of the Labor Unrest—the sudden class hatred, the unexpected violence, the irrational moods—makes it an essential, a sanguine, part of pre-war psychology, yet the immediate causes of it have a very different look. Grim and gray as they are, they direct us not to life but to death—to the unpleasantly decaying death of Liberal democracy.

*   *   *

It is impossible to say at exactly what date the doctrine of Syndicalism crept out of France across the English Channel. But it is generally conceded that it made this journey at some time between 1905 and 1910, and James Connolly, the Irish labor leader, is suspected of being responsible for its arrival. The journey was a short one, but it was difficult. Though Syndicalism means nothing more than "Trade Unionism" in French, it indicated a rather peculiar sort of Trade Unionism, and none the less peculiar—in the eyes of English workmen—for *being* French. It advocated the complete supremacy of the Trade Unions, which should federate themselves locally and centrally—a federation of local unions forming the local Authority, and a standing conference of national representatives of all the Trade Unions forming the National Authority. The producers, in other words, were to control all industries and all services; and they were to gain control through a violent succession of continuous strikes, culminating in a "general expropriatory Strike." Nothing, of course, could be more opposed to the collectivist theories of the Sidney Webbs, the Fabians, and the socialist members of the I.L.P., who foresaw, through a series of deliberate steps more or less divinely predestined by the Webbs themselves, the gradual evolution of the State into a great organization of consumers; and who, to be sure, are still foreseeing it.

Syndicalism had been a faith full-grown in France since 1902, and it had taken root among the immigrant population of the United States. In France the General Federation of Labor, in America the I.W.W. were in much the same position as the British Trade Unions had been in 1834—"a fearful engine of mischief," Dr. Arnold had called them in that year, "ready to riot or to assassinate." The *Syndicats* and the I.W.W. did, in fact, inspire a great deal of terror, nor is it to be supposed that any doctrine they might evolve would be quite so constructive as terroristic. As for the philosophy of Syndicalism, it was rooted in the anarchism of Nietzsche, had branched out into the *élan vital* of the Bergsonians, and finally come

to flower in the *Réflexions sur la Violence* of M. Sorel.

This strange philosophical growth could not—*qua* philosophy—have had the slightest appeal to British workmen. In the first place, they had probably never heard of Nietzsche or Bergson, and as for the *Réflexions sur la Violence* of M. Sorel they simply would not have understood them: in the second place, they were never very happy with a reasoned system of revolution. And yet, between 1910 and 1914, and against the wishes of their leaders, they plunged into a series of furious strikes which, but for the declaration of War, would have culminated in September, 1914, in a General Strike of extraordinary violence. The exact prescription for a syndicalist revolution.

How could this have come about? Could native thinkers have assisted them, re-stating the propositions of M. Sorel with all the passionate common-sense of the Anglo-Saxon tongue? One glance at the journalism of the day will prove that this could not be the case. *The Daily Herald* was a kind of intellectual ostrich, swallowing any and every wild idea, and disgorging them all, undigested, in a very unappetizing condition. *The New Age*, appalled at the apparent expulsion of all non-laboring intellectuals from the syndicalist world, was attempting to bridge the gulf with Guild Socialism, a mysterious combination of consumers and producers which the editor, Mr. A. R. Orage, may possibly have understood. *The Daily Citizen* still called for the old opportunist tactics. The language of *The Syndicalist* was vehement but obscure. *The New Statesman* preached, with a vigor which was highly laudable under the circumstances, the complacent fatalism of the Sidney Webbs. These may well have had their effect—a far from negligible effect—upon the younger intellectuals; but the mass of the workers they could not have reached at all.

Could it perhaps have been the agitations of Mr. Tom Mann, that ardent syndicalist, who, realizing that British workmen are not very susceptible to ideas, was determined to practice the ideas first and preach them afterwards? Mr. Tom Mann was one of the most successful and intelligent agitators in British labor history, but he was an effect rather than a cause of those four and a half strike years.

Or could it be that the air itself seemed full of agitated whispers, of echoes, and insinuations? From America and France there came, sea-borne like a sound of bells, the reverberations of a violent attack upon political democracy. From the rare, cold upper regions of economic speculation there drifted down, as light as snow and scarcely comprehended, a disturbing rumor that conditions would never improve in a capitalist world, that indeed they must inevitably grow worse. And a question, airy but insistent, poised itself on the edges of conscious thought: had not a combination of science and reform, by insisting on healthier conditions of labor and life, made more workers physically "available" for longer periods of their existence? made them, in effect, cheaper and cheaper commodities in the labor market? Already, though hardly visible as yet in the general activity, an increasing horde of the casually employed, the unemployed, and the unemployable drifted through the country.

These reasons are forcible enough, but they do not answer the main question— How did these strike years come to be conducted, tactically, on purely syndicalist lines?

The majority of British workers were involved in the strikes, sympathetically if not actively; there is no doubt of that: and yet the majority of British workers, in the two elections of 1910, obediently voted either Liberal or Conservative, preserved —in their political consciousness—an almost theological reverence for the operations of Parliament, and would have been dismayed at the very mention of the word "revolution." How could they express—as they did—an increasing, an unprecedented class hatred? how could they shake—as they did—the very foundations of parlia-

mentary rule? how could they be at once syndicalist and not syndicalist, revolutionary and not revolutionary? The answer may be found in a phrase of Mr. Fabian Ware's, a Conservative writer, who in *The Worker and His Country* asserted that syndicalism was "an assertion of instinct against reason"—in other words, a convenient expression for a new energy. Women's Suffrage was also a convenient expression for a new energy and so was the slogan "Ulster will fight and Ulster will be right." . . .

The instinct of the British worker was very active in 1910. It warned him that he was underpaid, that Parliament—left to itself—would keep him underpaid; it told him that good behavior had ceased to have any meaning; it asserted that he must unite at all costs. The only visible symbol of unity was the Trade Unions: to the Trade Unions therefore he turned.

And the Trade Unions became the not too willing repository for instincts, for feelings, for a kind of vital unreason.

The first steps into the Unrest seem straightforward enough—anger at the fall of real wages, at capitalist aggression, at the unwillingness of Parliament; anger fomented by agitators, and informed by vague fears, and leading to solidarity. One step more, and we reach the Trade Unions; and suddenly there lies before us, in darkness and confusion, a labyrinth of contradictory paths. Revolutionary methods appear, but not revolutionary intentions; distrust of and respect for political democracy are hopelessly intermingled; the Government is simultaneously attacked and defended, and by the same people; reason wars with instinct. Can one discern at last, after the dark journey through those complicated mazes, the deployment for a mighty battle—in which Capital, already organized through the operation of inhuman and infallible laws, is pitted against the Unions, the fallible armies of human beings?

It would be very convenient to think so. But the battle, though it had begun far back in the nineteenth century, though it proclaimed itself in every strike and from every platform, was reserved in all its fury for the post-war world. Between the two armies there interposes itself, waving a worm-eaten olive-branch, the complacent presence of the Liberal Government, combining in its person at once the majesty of Parliament, the allurements of reform, and the solid weight of constitutional respectability. Is it really an economic battle, then, which will be found at the heart of the labyrinth? or can one take one turn more, creep around one more corner, and discover an even deeper, an even more human, conflict?

For the assaults upon Parliament of the Tories, the women, and the workers have something profoundly in common. In each case, a certain conscious security was in question. As for the workers, it must be remembered that their life was not—in 1910—at all invaded by despair, by the post-war certainty that things would never,

by any chance, get very much better. The majority of people did not think in economics then, but in politics. In 1910, an industrious man might still believe that he had a chance of improving himself, and that his children and his grandchildren would climb higher rather than descend as the years went on. And yet that smothering security, implied in the phrase "a fair day's pay for a fair day's work," had to be overthrown; it was the very essence of Victorian respectability, and the ultimate expression of it was parliamentary mediation. The workers did not want to be safe any more; they wanted to live, to take chances, to throw caution to the winds: they had been repressed too long. And so the deepest impulse in the great strike movement of 1910-1914 was an unconscious one, an enormous energy pressing up from the depths of the soul; and Parliament shuddered before it, and under its impact Liberal England died.

II. DISINTEGRATION OF THE PARTY AFTER 1914?

Dissolved Under Impact of War

TREVOR WILSON

The Liberal party may have had ailments before 1914, says Trevor Wilson, but it is impossible for the historian to say that they were fatal diseases. He can only know with certainty that the party entered the war in a state of apparent health, and expired soon after. The "most warrantable guess," therefore, is that the death blow was delivered during the conflict. In his presentation Wilson studies the impact of the war upon various sections of the party. His thesis is drawn from these observations.

THE OUTBREAK of the First World War initiated a process of disintegration in the Liberal party which by 1918 had reduced it to ruins. As Liberals were often the first to recognise, the onset of war jeopardised the existence of a party whose guiding principles were international conciliation, personal liberty, and social reform. On the fateful 4th of August 1914 Christopher Addison, a junior member of the Liberal government, foretold his party's demise in words which, with one variation or another, were to be repeated many times in the following years. Addison was talking with Sir John Simon, the Attorney-General, about possible resignations from the government, and Simon said that he was reluctant to see too many ministers resign because that would necessitate a coalition government, "which would assuredly be the grave of Liberalism." Addison gloomily replied that in the opinion of most Liberals, and certainly of himself, Liberalism was in its grave already. A few months later a prominent Scottish Liberal wrote privately: "I meet many good Liberals in Midlothian and elsewhere who are prone to take the view that we pacifists made a mistake and the Jingos were right all along."

For a Liberal government to lead Britain into war, and to direct a wartime administration, seemed almost a contradiction in terms. Its task of international pacification had automatically disappeared. And it had little hope of preserving intact those principles and practices identified with Liberalism: free trade, protection of minorities, the "pacification" of Ireland, liberty of the individual, and voluntary service in the armed forces. Yet once a Liberal government began to modify its ideals under stress of war, how long would it be before the liberal position was abandoned altogether and that of the Conservatives adopted? In short, war and the conduct of war threatened to eliminate liberalism as a coherent political position.

From Trevor Wilson, *The Downfall of the Liberal Party 1914–1935* (London, 1966). Reprinted by permission of Collins Publishers and Cornell University Press, pp. 23–48.

While some liberal principles were being suspended for the duration, others seemed unlikely (except to devout Liberals) ever to become important again. Issues on which Liberals possessed a distinctive and militant attitude, like temperance, denominational education, and Welsh Church disestablishment, suddenly seemed irrelevant both now and for the future. The one attempt made to further temperance as a cause during the war failed ignominiously, and an Education Act was passed in 1918 without a whisper of the denominational controversies which had once roused Liberals. As for the central liberal tenet of free trade, even individualistic Liberals like J. M. Robertson and Lord Murray of Elibank began to doubt its revival. Murray in 1916 warned a director of the Liberal *Westminster Gazette* that the paper should avoid discussing "whether or not we should trade with the Germans after the war."

Personally [he wrote] I think that as the Emperor William has been responsible for our adopting conscription, so may he be responsible for our changing all our tariff traditions and our adopting a commercial imperial federation working in association with the Allied Powers. At any rate, I would advise the paper to be very cautious in committing itself to any opinions on tariffs at this stage. The prosecution of the war and a consolidated Government at home are the only policies which the mass of the public demands.

On these questions which alone concerned "the mass of the public" there was no distinctive liberal position, and no standard round which the party could rally.

As "the prosecution of the war" pushed aside liberal issues, so it undermined the organisations associated with the Liberal party. By 1918 the powerful forces within the Irish and Labour movements which favoured co-operation with the Liberals, so providing Asquith with a parliamentary majority between 1910 and 1914, had been disrupted. Even more serious was the damage suffered by the great force of religious Nonconformity. Charles Royle, a Stockport butcher of humble origin who was deeply involved in Nonconformist and temperance activities, has written of one branch of Nonconformity, the National Brotherhood movement:

When the war commenced in 1914 our members began to join up and before it was finished over 600 had been enrolled as serving the King.

We found to our great regret that it was one thing for them to go and although the big majority came back to the town [Stockport] only a small number resumed their membership of the Brotherhood. Is it to be wondered at, after the devastating influences of such an experience, that men should have little room for things of a religious nature.

Nonconformity, it should be stressed, was not just a pressure group which looked to the Liberals for aid on some issues. Its religious dynamic expressed itself in political terms. One of its chief periodicals, the *British Weekly* (edited by Sir William Robertson Nicoll), called itself "a journal of social and Christian progress." Nonconformity had seen the Liberal party as the instrument, politically, of "social and Christian progress," and Liberalism had correspondingly been underpinned by the force of Nonconformist conviction. But central to the Free Church ideal of "Christian progress" was peace between nations. As the *British Weekly* said on 6 August 1914: "We of the Free Churches are bound under the most tremendous penalties to set the example of peace and good will." It had long been clear, it continued, that the present military system of Europe must come to an end, either by general disarmament, or by mutual destruction. "The Free Churches have worked for disarmament, and who can blame them?" In this way they had hoped that this bloodshed, this devastation, this outbreak of deadly passions, these strong perils casting their shadows far into the future, might be averted.

The purpose of this article was not to urge neutrality, but to explain the necessity for intervening in the war. Yet the terms in which it was expressed suggested the blow which Nonconformity had suffered. (A few days earlier, before the violation of Belgium, Robertson Nicoll had written to Lloyd George utterly opposing intervention). At the beginning of December 1914 Sir George Riddell, the newspaper owner, found Nicoll "very broken by the war. He said that he had been at a Free Church meeting on Friday and that some of the dissenting ministers are still peace-at-any-price people. On the other hand, some are very militant. For example, one wanted Nicoll to insert in the *British Weekly* a little story of which the point was that we should pray for the destruction of the Germans." These differences disintegrated Nonconformity, especially as a political force. Whereas by 1918 prominent divines like Maude Royden were moving over to the Labour party, others like Dr. Shakespeare had followed Lloyd George into Conservative company. Nicoll took the latter course. He even, in December 1914, favoured inserting the dubious paragraph about praying for the destruction of the Germans. Thereafter he strongly advocated severe restrictions on enemy aliens, conscription for the armed forces, and a Lloyd George premiership—all of them causes associated with the Conservatives rather than the Liberals. By June 1915 his journal was being spoken of in the same breath as Lord Northcliffe's *Times*. Haldane wrote to his mother: "The 'Times' is now joining with the 'British Weekly' in a movement to turn out the poor P.M. & substitute Ll. George." When Nicoll died in 1923, Lloyd George spoke of him warmly as a good friend and a great help during the war. The two of them, Lloyd George said ("with much bitterness"), had made enemies because when they decided—reluctantly—to go into the war they went in heart and soul, whereas other Liberals agreed to participate but sought to satisfy their anti-war proclivities by carrying on the struggle in a meagre and unsatisfactory way. (Significantly, Lloyd George here seemed to be using "Liberals"

as synonymous with "Nonconformists"). To Lloyd George, Nicoll's attitude had been vitally important in securing Free Church support for the war, and so in deciding the outcome of the conflict.

But if the war effort had prospered, Nonconformity had been the loser. It had become too closely associated with a regime Conservative in complexion and nationalistic in outlook. Whereas the Church of England might survive, and even prosper from, identification with the nation in arms, such identification did violence to the genius of Nonconformity. Yet those Free Churchmen who resisted this trend seemed helpless to save their cause. They had struggled so hard to avert war that with the outbreak of hostilities they had lost their bearings, and almost their *raison d' être*. J. Allen Baker, who was a leading Quaker, a London social reformer, and a Liberal M.P., is a case in point. Before 1914 his unremitting efforts had been devoted increasingly to international conciliation, and in this cause he had travelled widely and been welcomed by the Kaiser, the American President, and the British Foreign Secretary. Then in August 1914 his world collapsed about him. From being a considerable force in the land he became a quite unimportant figure. He died in 1918, heartbroken and almost forgotten. In a sense the fate of Nonconformity was the fate of the Liberal party.

II

For the Conservative and Labour parties, these years presented no such menace. From the outset the war redounded to the advantage of the Conservatives. It seemed to vindicate their pre-war conduct, particularly their hostility to Germany, their advocacy of a tariff policy directed (amongst other things) against German trade, and their demand for increased armaments and peacetime conscription. Further, the war produced in Britain a mood of acute, sometimes frenzied, nationalism which was bound to help the Conservatives as being the more nationalistic, "patriotic" party. And the actual conduct of war demanded encroachments on the liberty of the individual which were more acceptable to Conservatives than to Liberals; for, as the *Manchester Guardian* said on May 8, 1916, love of personal freedom was of the essence of liberalism, and resort to compulsion in accord with the traditions of conservatism.

Initially Labour secured no comparable advantage from the war. The party was divided into a majority supporting British intervention and a minority, including the I.L.P. section, opposing it. Its internal dissensions on this matter, and its "internationalist" outlook in the past, cost it many adherents, to whom it now seemed insufficiently patriotic. These losses led, among other things, to the formation of the right-wing British Workers League (later called the National Democratic party), which captured Merthyr Tydfil from Labour at a by-election in November 1915. C. B. Stanton, the victor in this contest, had formerly been a Labour candidate and miners' leader. And J. A. Seddon, who became chairman of the National Democratic party, had been a Labour M.P. and chairman of the T.U.C. not long before.

Yet the war proved in the long run of the greatest benefit to Labour. In the first place, it wrought such havoc upon the Liberals that it provided Labour, as the party nearest them in political complexion, with the chance to appropriate their position of principal left-wing party. Despite the small importance of the pre-war Labour party, it proved of the utmost advantage for it simply to have existed in 1914—existed, that is, as a parliamentary, non-revolutionary party with important, if still limited, trade union associations and with many attributes of radical Nonconformity. As a consequence the Liberal party only had to suffer a shattering disaster for Labour to take over its role as chief contender for office with the Conservatives.

The war not only inflicted such a disaster on the Liberals but provided Labour with the impetus to seize its opportunity. The impact of the war on the nation's economy so increased the importance of the trade unions, and so stimulated their political consciousness, that it correspondingly enhanced the position of the Labour party, which had all along derived much of its limited importance from its association with organised labour. Primarily it was not the numerical strength of the Labour party in the House of Commons or the calibre of its members available for office, but the need for trade union co-operation in the war, which caused Labour to receive posts in the wartime coalitions. Certainly if Labour's following in the House of Commons alone was considered, it had little claim to equal representation with the Liberals in Lloyd George's five-man war cabinet. What secured it this position was its enhanced political potential, resulting from its connection with the trade union movement.

Participation in these wartime governments did not, moreover, deprive Labour of what was to be a prime advantage after the war: freedom from responsibility for the deeds of governments up to that time. Labour had supported the Asquith administration before the war, and from 1915 to 1918 held office in the coalitions, yet it was only marginally associated with these governments. Indeed during the war it combined membership of them with independence of, and even hostility to, the other parties making them up. In the short term Labour was to suffer for its detachment from Lloyd George's "victorious" administration. But in the long run it was to prove an advantage that, unlike the Liberals, Labour was not directly responsible for the alleged errors or misdeeds of the past. In consequence many of those who thought the British government in some measure culpable for the outbreak of war, or who hoped to redeem the sacrifices of the war by constructing a new social order, abandoned the Liberals as supposedly tranished by failure and threw in their lot with Labour.

III

The way in which the onset and conduct of war disrupted the Liberals may be shown by the behaviour of various sections of the party. The allegiance of one group was irrevocably shaken by the decision to participate at all. The war to them was not the product of German militarism but of "pre-war diplomacy," a system which they equated with the balance of power, armaments-building, and binding agreements between rival power groupings. In their view, Britain's Liberal government had gravely erred by joining in this system, and so had helped to bring about the war. As one Liberal "pacifist" M.P., Philip Morrell (employing all the judiciousness he could summon up), put the matter in October 1916:

I was opposed to the policy of the Triple Entente, which in my judgment was one of the principal causes leading to war, and so far from thinking that the outbreak can be attributed entirely to the exceptional wickedness of one nation or one man, I held, and still hold, that whatever may have been the special guilt of Germany, which I do not for a moment extenuate or excuse, all the Governments of the Great Powers of Europe, not excluding our own, were in different degrees responsible for the outbreak.

For these Liberals, the impending subjugation of Western Europe by German militarism in August 1914 was no sufficient ground for intervening in the war. According to P. A. Molteno, "no vital interest" of Britain "has been attacked." According to Joseph King, Britain was obliged to "protest" against the German assault on Belgium but not to go to Belgium's aid. In the opinion of the British Neutrality League (a body formed on the eve of war and including several Liberal M.P.s) there was no likelihood that Germany would annex Belgium, and if it did so this would only make Germany "weaker than she is now, for she would have to use all her forces for holding her conquests down." In any case, as Arnold Rowntree put it, if Britain did intervene successfully against Germany, Russian despotism would become dominant in Europe.

Underlying this extraordinary mixture of high-mindedness, self-interest, and wild delusion was the conviction that neither the circumstances in which Germany

attacked in 1914, nor the military victories likely to follow, should influence Liberals on the question of intervention. According to Arthur Ponsonby, the British case set out in the White Paper on the outbreak of war was overwhelming. But the causes of the war were not to be found in the events related there. They went much farther back, to a policy with which he had profoundly disagreed—a policy of armaments, the balance of power, and secret diplomacy. It was, he claimed, a diplomats' not a people's war.

It is little wonder that Liberals taking this view, and believing that their leaders had helped to cause the war, became disillusioned with their party. (It is also not surprising that the M.P.s in this group were often repudiated by the Liberal associations in their constituencies). Not all of them ceased to be Liberals; a small section, usually wedded like Francis Hirst and Arnold Lupton to *laissez-faire* economics, remained in the party as a dissident, critical element. Others, including Lord Morley and John Burns who resigned from the cabinet on the question of intervention, drifted out of politics altogether. "For the moment," Morley wrote to a Liberal editor in 1915, "our common ground on public things is broken to pieces. We don't speak the same language." But by far the greater section of Liberal "pacifists" remained politically active yet severed their ties with the Liberal party. In the next few years C. P. Trevelyan (who also left the government in August 1914), Ponsonby, King, C. R. Buxton, and H. B. Lees-Smith transferred their allegiance to Labour and became openly hostile to the Liberals.

IV

As it happened, the number of Liberal "pacifists" at the outbreak of war proved much smaller than seemed probable only two or three days before. As the left-wing periodical the *Nation* said on October 17, 1914: "the policy of the British Government receives a more whole-hearted and reasoned support than has been given to the policy of any war that has ever been waged by the nation." "Radicals, Socialists, and Syndicalists," it went on, had been rallied to support of the war by the events leading to its outbreak. As war spread across Europe "internationalist" Liberals like Josiah Wedgwood and Gilbert Murray, and radical journals like the *Nation* and *Manchester Guardian,* were shocked out of a neutralist attitude by "the stupefying panorama of German arrogance" and the prospect of "brute force" overrunning Europe. In Wedgwood's view, social reformers had been called from their task by a more elementary battle for liberty, and if that battle was lost everything they cared for would be lost with it.

But not all Liberals who took this view in 1914 held to it thereafter. Doubts about the Liberal government's responsibility for the coming of war, banished for the moment, sometimes revived as the events of August 1914 became obscured by the carnage of the next four years, and as the claims of Liberals who attributed the war to "secret diplomacy" gained rather specious verification from the publication of the wartime secret treaties by the Russian Bolsheviks. Moreover, many of the Liberals who had reluctantly agreed to British intervention were at one with the "pacifists" regarding the methods by which the war should be conducted. They held that Britain must fight the war on the basis of liberal principles, and that the abandonment of these principles would constitute a triumph for "prussianism." So while they might not accept Morrell's views about responsibility for the war, they frequently agreed with him about the principles which should govern wartime administration. Liberals, he said in the speech of 1916 already quoted, should not abandon in this conflict the principles of individual liberty—free trade, free service, freedom of opinion—which had made Britain one of the best-governed and most prosperous countries in the world. And he went on:

The system of conscription, like the system of [Tariff] Protection, with which it is closely allied, is in every country where it exists one of the most potent instruments of privilege and oppression. It gives to the military authorities a power over the lives of other men, and especially the lives of the workers, which is destructive of all true progress. It leads inevitably to that spirit of militarism of which the pernicious effects, as developed in Germany, are now very visible to us.

Many non-pacifist Liberals agreed with him about upholding liberal ideals in wartime. This can be seen (if in exaggerated form) from the attitude of W. M. R. Pringle and J. M. Hogge, the "terrible twins" who harried Lloyd George in the later years of the war. Both Pringle and Hogge supported British intervention. Pringle, speaking in Parliament on August 3, 1914 following the German ultimatum to Belgium, dissociated himself from former colleagues like Ponsonby. In the coming conflict between blood and iron and international morality, he said, those holding to liberal traditions must take the side of morality. His speech was considered important, as pointing to the abandonment of neutralism by many Liberal M.P.s because of the threat to Belgium. Yet although supporters of the war, he and Hogge stoutly resisted, first under Asquith and then under Lloyd George, measures of compulsion and restrictions on personal freedom. Even something as mild as a proposal by the Liberal government, early in 1915, to take the whole time of the House of Commons aroused their ire as infringing the rights of private members. Why would the government not trust them, Hogge demanded, when they were all trying their level best to support it in the great issues in which it was involved. The government, he complained, "take no notice of private Members of this House and of their own supporters—an excellent Liberal example." And he added, with no little exaggeration: "I would remind the Prime Minister that already the Cabinet have shut the mouth of the Press in this country, and they are now proposing to shut the mouths of private Members in this House."

To Liberals of this way of thinking, Asquith during the first two years of the war was guilty of repeated deviations from the liberal position: in the sphere of personal liberty by the Defence of the Realm Act and the press censorship, in the sphere of government by the admission of a Conservative element, including Sir Edward Carson, into the ministry, in the sphere of free trade by the McKenna duties of 1915 and the "Paris Resolutions" of 1916, in the sphere of Ireland by the mismanagement which led up to and followed the Easter Rebellion of 1916, and above all in the sphere of voluntary service by the resort to conscription. To Liberal fundamentalists the war was no excuse for these actions. They denied, as Simon did when he resigned from the government over conscription, that any serious deficiency in the war effort existed under the voluntary system; and if shown that deficiencies did exist they were prepared to argue, as did Reginald McKenna and Walter Runciman while resisting conscription in the cabinet, that the whole concept of total war implicit in the measure meant a struggle beyond Britain's resources. Pringle, taking up a contrast which Asquith had made between his government and that of the younger Pitt, asserted:

if Pitt and his successors were successful it was because they, in spite of all criticism, in spite of all failures, in spite of all complaints, adhered with the utmost strictness to the traditional policy of this country, namely, never to enter upon a Continental war on the basis of unlimited military liability. That we have done in the present case.

It is clear that Liberals of this school had not wholly overcome their misgivings about Britain's involvement in war. Initially they had not appreciated how large a sacrifice of liberal principles it might entail. On theoretical grounds they would scarcely admit that the war could be conducted more effectively by compulsory than by voluntary means. And where their view was successfully challenged, they were so alarmed by the danger of permanent restrictions on liberty that they preferred, however they might rationalise their attitude, that the conduct of the war should suffer.

Consequently as the war proceeded an increasing number of Liberals began condemning their leaders, and indeed their party as a whole, for "betraying" liberal ideals. And they often inquired despairingly whether Liberalism would ever rise again after such misfortunes—queries which followed on directly from the doubts expressed on the outbreak of war about Liberalism's powers of survival. Lady Toulmin, wife of an M.P., wrote in mid-1916 that it was difficult for a life-long Liberal to speak with moderation about the state of Liberal politics. Unity had been maintained in the government by the surrender of all their party held dear: a voluntary army, the right of asylum, respect for conscience, education, Home Rule, and international law as touching the rights of neutrals. Other parties had surrendered nothing and had gained all along the line. "Will it," she asked, "need another twenty years in the wilderness to purify and purge the Liberal party of the poison it has swallowed with such docility during the last months?" For many a year, she concluded, "there shall be doubt, disappointment, and pain; never glad, confident morning again." These statements, affirmed the president of the women's Liberal organisation in Yorkshire, expressed the view of thousands of sincere rank and file Liberals, who had been rendered dumb by recent events but were eagerly awaiting an opportunity to battle for the principles of faith. Some of them were asking whether they could honestly remain associated with a party whose sanction had been given to active work against liberal principles.

Not all the Liberals who took this pessimistic view went so far as to abandon the party. Pringle and Hogge served out their political careers as Liberals, the former becoming reconciled to Asquith after the war, the latter remaining hostile to the end. But whether or not they left the party, they weakened it by endorsing the view that it was no longer a fit custodian of liberal principles. A party whose shortcomings were so loudly proclaimed by its own adherents had little chance of keeping its following intact or securing the allegiance of new entrants to politics—especially when another party unblemished by these supposed lapses was seeking to replace the Liberals as the principal left-wing party.

v

So far attention has been directed to the Liberals whose allegiance was shaken by the decision to go to war or by the methods employed to conduct it. But another section turned against the party for precisely opposite reasons: because they considered it unwilling to surrender traditional ideas in face of the clear demands of war. To this group, the war and its efficient conduct took precedence over all other questions, including the principles of their party. And efficiency to them involved those measures of state direction and compulsion advocated by Conservatives and resisted by orthodox Liberals—measures like conscription for the armed forces, coercion of trade unions, punitive action against conscientious objectors and enemy aliens, and abandonment of free trade. Further, they were not prepared to wait for these measures while other Liberals were being convinced of their necessity. They wanted them immediately, even if it meant alienating the mass of Liberals and making an alliance with the Conservatives. Whereas most Liberals who supported the war tried to make their liberalism and their "patriotism" march hand in hand, or anyway to sacrifice only as much of their liberalism as the needs of patriotism absolutely demanded, many in this group did not. By placing the war before everything else they in effect abandoned their liberalism, moving over, in their ideology, their policy, and their political associations, into the Conservative camp.

No one made this transition more wholeheartedly than Lloyd George. For him the change was considerable. Although never peace-at-any-price, he had resisted intervention in August 1914. On August 3 one of his fellow ministers, C. F. G. Masterman, "spoke strongly of the way in which George had fought in the Cabinet all through the week for peace." And Lloyd George himself said that he "had done his utmost for peace but events had been too strong for him." He had even declined to treat a minor violation of Belgium as a *casus belli,* and it was only the full-scale invasion which had ended his resistance.

But once Lloyd George (like Robertson Nicoll) was in the war he would admit of no half-measures. As he wrote a few years later: "it was not 'my war'. . . . But being in it, I realised that the only safe way out was through the gates of victory, and that victory was only to be won by concentrating all thought and energy on the making of war." The truth was that the struggle obsessed him. He showed utter disregard for military leaders who (in his view) failed to comprehend the needs of the war as well as he did: hence his conflicts with Lord Kitchener, Admiral Jellicoe, Field-Marshal Haig, and Sir William Robertson. And he rejected out of hand liberal practices and principles—not to mention Liberal statesmen—when he considered them a hindrance to the war effort. Whereas Asquith showed little relish for the measures of compulsion he felt obliged to introduce, Lloyd George was not at all squeamish. Sometimes he made a peremptory effort to reconcile support for conscription with belief in liberalism, as when he claimed that the great battles for liberty in the past, like the French Revolutionary wars and the American Civil War, had been fought by conscript armies. But as the *Manchester Guardian* (a paper generally sympathetic to him) pointed out on May 8, 1916, what worried Liberals was not that he eventually supported conscription but that he had adopted it too readily, and had not appeared averse to doing so.

That is, he had seemed prone to rely on force rather than persuasion, and to substitute compulsion for organisation. In so doing he had moved away from the liberal and towards the conservative position. What was more, although the *Manchester Guardian* did not say this, he had moved into the company of Conservatives and of those right-wing Liberals seeking an understanding with the Conservatives, and had not appeared anxious to conciliate the left-wing Liberals with whom he had once been associated.

In the long run, the defection of these Liberals who were prepared to abandon a liberal position and ally themselves with the Conservatives was probably less damaging than the withdrawal of members claiming that Liberalism had been betrayed by its leaders. Many in the conscriptionist group were untypical of the party as a whole, comprising what *The Times* on December 13, 1916 called "the substantial men in the party": members of landed and political families like Winston Churchill and F. E. Guest, mill and mine owners like Sir Arthur Markham and Sir Frederick Cawley, commercial figures who had become newspaper owners like Sir Henry Dalziel, and leading members of the chemical industry like Sir Alfred Mond. (The disproportionately large number of recipients of titles in this group may have been connected with the award of honours to persons who contributed substantially to party funds). The breaking-away of this group, like the secession of the whigs in the 1880s, was most injurious to the party —and not least to its finances—but not mortally wounding. It was less dangerous to lose a group moving from liberalism to conservatism than to lose radicals who claimed that they were preserving their principles unimpaired, and leaving the party in order to safeguard them.

Yet the withdrawal of the former section still did the party a great deal of damage. By their advocacy of sterner measures in prosecuting the war, and their demand for more dynamic leadership than Asquith provided, they won at least partial assent from many Liberals who, though unhappy about allying with the Conservatives, agreed that a major war could not be conducted by established liberal methods or the established Liberal leader. Further, although their defection robbed the party of only two of its most prominent individuals, namely Lloyd George and Churchill, they were the two on whom (according to Halévy) "the eyes of the public were fixed" before the war, "the men of tomorrow" as Asquith had appeared to be only a man of the present. And Lloyd George's defection rendered the radical section leaderless for the second time in thirty-five years, depriving it once again of the man whom it had regarded as its particular spokesman—"the Radical leader," as the *Nation* sadly described him, "to whom democracy was accustomed to look as its representative man."

VI

While the war was dissolving the allegiance of Liberals on both the left and right of the party, it was reducing the remainder to near-helplessness. Faithful to Liberalism, they yet could see no way to stave off the disaster threatening it, and often seemed to lack even the will-power to act on its behalf. Their impotence was in sharp contrast to the growing assertiveness not only of the leaders but even more the rank and file of the Conservative and Labour parties.

Fundamentally this loss of initiative sprang from an inability to reconcile liberal ideals with effective prosecution of the war. But the difficulties of Liberals were aggravated by the behaviour of Asquith and his closest associates, both as leaders of the party and as directors of the war effort. Most Liberals were prepared to sacrifice their principles when the necessities of war imperatively demanded it. But too often Asquith seemed to call for such sacrifices less on account of the military situation than because of acute political pressure threatening his government. While some Liberals were prepared to accept his lead on all occasions, others could not overlook the political manœuvring which so often preceded his departures from a liberal position.

There was a further cause of misgiving among Liberals which had nothing to do with political principle or party allegiance: the question of Asquith's fitness as war leader. The war did not go well during his premiership; failure attended the Allied effort in Gallipoli and Mesopotamia, on the Russian front and the western front, in Serbia and Roumania. Even some of his supporters considered him partly responsible for these setbacks. His wartime administrations seemed wanting in foresight and energy, and he did not create the impression of being a visionary, dynamic leader. Nor were these misgivings confined to advocates of compulsion or opponents of the Liberal party. The diary of the radical Addison reveals how, during the first year of the war, his admiration for Asquith was changed first to uneasiness and then to antipathy by what seemed his leader's habitual fumbling and indecision.

For Liberals occupying this middle position—anxious both for their party and for the war, and doubtful of Asquith either as custodian of liberal principles or as director of the national effort—no line of action seemed open. Should they assail the government on some outstanding issue, they would bring Asquith down, for without Liberal support he was unlikely to survive a day. Notwithstanding the presence of the Conservative leaders in his government from May 1915, he enjoyed no real following among the Conservative rank and file. Only because he was leader of the Liberal party, and because it was difficult to envisage a ministry being formed without Liberal support, did he retain office for so long. Nor did he hesitate to threaten resignation if his followers became too restive. The party was profoundly shaken in May 1915 by his decision, at Conservative insistence, to form a coalition ministry; it required a twenty-minute exhortation from him to dissuade a meeting of over a hundred Liberal M.P.s from passing a resolution hostile to the change. On this occasion he warned them quite frankly that if the resolution was adopted he would leave office. And the same threat, even if not explicitly repeated, faced his followers whenever they felt like challenging his actions.

The difficulty of Liberals in this situation was stated by one M.P. during the upheaval over the first conscription bill. H. W. Massingham, the editor of the *Nation,* had written bitterly that only thirty of the "200 Liberal Anti-Conscriptionist members" had actually voted against the bill, and this M.P., signing himself "One of the 200," put the case for those who had not. If all of them had voted against conscription, he said, Asquith would have resigned and Lloyd George taken his place, and Massingham himself had said that this should be avoided. The party had been foolish to tie its hands by agreeing to a coalition, but it would be even more foolish to commit suicide by forcing Asquith to resign over conscription.

Fear of unseating Asquith lest a worse fate befall them played a signal part in reducing the Liberals to impotence during the early years of the war. At first sight it seems surprising that neither Massingham nor "One of the 200" rejoiced at the prospect of Lloyd George as Premier, considering his qualities of wartime leadership. But he combined these qualities with others less attractive to Liberals: blatant disloyalty to his colleagues, open intriguing for office, and a ready acceptance of compulsion and Conservative allies. Only great disgust with Asquith would cause "middle" Liberals to consider replacing him by Lloyd George. A few did so. The *Manchester Guardian,* claiming that the war must take paramountcy over party or person and that Asquith was ill-equipped as war leader, welcomed Lloyd George as Premier. Indeed, it had called on him seven months earlier to abandon the government and join Churchill and Carson in opposition. Yet when he eventually became Prime Minister, even this newspaper admitted to a pang

of regret at seeing him leading a largely
Conservative government. It warned him
—as it proved, in vain—"to walk warily and
to permit no sort of provocation, should
provocation come, to goad him into antagonism to the party to which he still owes
allegiance, and to preserve for the future
of Liberalism all the treasure of his soul."

Many Liberals who agreed generally
with the *Manchester Guardian* and even
endorsed its strictures against Asquith,
felt that the dangers of a Conservative-
dominated government under Lloyd
George were too great to justify a change
of ministry. Nor was it only party prejudice which caused this attitude. They
feared that once in power the Conservatives would use the war to attain objectives
deeply repugnant to them: permanent
curtailments on liberty, coercive measures
against labour, the final alienation of Ireland, imperialistic war aims, and a punitive
peace settlement. Nor could Liberals welcome a change of government which in
part would be attributable to the defama-
tory, rabble-rousing, fundamentally anti-
democratic tactics of the press barons, and
which might advance those individuals towards political power. In the event not all
of their fears were to be realised. But the
Conservative party's behaviour in the pre-
war years and during the first years of the
war makes it difficult to claim that any of
them were groundless.

The essential helplessness of Liberals
who regretted Asquith's performance yet
feared his supersession is illustrated by a
Nation article called "The Coalition and
After," written on the eve of his fall. "We
are afraid," it said of the Asquith coalition,
". . . that from the first it proclaimed its
unfitness for the task." All through it had
been a "mere mechanical combination of
Front Bench men" fettered by party interests and personal susceptibilities, with Asquith acting as a kind of referee seeking
compromises between opposing principles.
The nation was in no mood for delay. It
would insist on a change of method, and
would respect no one, from the Prime

Minister down, who failed to provide it.
Yet this article did not go on to demand a
new administration, but to warn against
any likely replacement. The Asquith coalition was a "poor, uninspired" government,
but its successor might be worse—not so
much in ability as in character. And it
asked:

What precisely does the country expect from
the type of politician who has followed the
strange banner that has been raised now from
the centre of the ranks of the Coalition, and
now from the circumference [i.e. by Lloyd
George and Carson respectively]? A strong or
a united Cabinet? A satisfied Army? A well-
ordered plan of campaign? A good peace? A
contented Alliance? A resettled Europe? There
is no such prospect.

For Liberals who felt like this, there was
no way of escape. They could only look on,
with growing despair and no real will to
resist, as their party disintegrated and forces
hostile to it wrested power from the failing
hands of Asquith and his semi-Liberal
regime.

VII

This survey of the effects of the war on
the Liberal party would not be complete if
it was confined to the rank and file. For
the war also had a most adverse effect on
the party's upper strata. In a number of
ways it helped to disrupt the group of individuals who made up the Liberal leadership, destroying the reputations of some
and providing others with the chance to
enhance their positions by allying with
their party's enemies, so creating profound
distrust between former close associates.
Hence by the end of the war the Liberal
leadership, as a reasonably coherent body
of individuals working generally together
in the interests of the party, had ceased to
exist. Such leaders as the party retained
were either elder statesmen apparently no
longer in touch with the pressing issues of
politics, or younger figures who had failed
in the testing experience of the war. Those
prominent Liberals who had improved their
standing had also apparently severed their

links with the man body of their party.

The extent to which this development injured Liberalism, and for that matter the part played by prominent individuals in the triumphs and failures of political parties, is open to dispute. But few would doubt that the disintegration of the body of outstanding leaders which the Liberal party possessed in 1914 was of substantial importance in its loss of confidence and public support. The defection of Lloyd George alone wrought it great harm. He had been heir apparent to the Liberal leadership and a driving force behind the social reforming movement in the pre-war Liberal government, and it was particularly damaging that he should become an object of distrust among Liberals who had been his personal followers and large sections of organised labour once sympathetic to his brand of liberalism. In part their antipathy was the result of his eager adoption, as explained earlier, of measures repugnant to orthodox Liberals. But this is not the whole explanation. Lloyd George, it appeared to many Liberals, welcomed the Tory embrace for its own sake, and not merely because he saw in Tory ideas the best way of winning the war; welcomed it, that is, because he realised that by forming an alliance with the Conservatives he could unseat Asquith and seize the premiership. In short, Liberal hostility sprang largely from the conviction that he was conspiring with the enemies of his party for his personal advantage.

What is to be said of this? In the first place it is unnecessary to believe that Asquith fell from office simply because of an intrigue between Lloyd George and the right-wing press. Whatever Asquith's abilities as a wartime administrator, even some of his colleagues were critical of him. McKenna, usually considered a prime Asquithian (certainly he loathed Lloyd George), nevertheless voiced misgivings about his chief: he was reported in April 1916 as speaking of Asquith's "failure to come to decisions," and as saying "that he would favour a change in the head of the

Government if he could see an alternative." Curzon, a Conservative member of the first coalition who also disliked Lloyd George, wrote during the crisis of December 1916: "we know that with [Asquith] as Chairman, either of the Cabinet or War Committee, it is absolutely impossible to win the War." And Edmund Gosse, only a month before Asquith's fall, related that "one of [Asquith's] closest friends told me last night [that the Prime Minister] plays bridge *three times a day*!" Now even if this information was correct, it might mean no more than that Asquith found in bridge-playing the relaxation which Churchill in a later war secured by after-lunch naps. But clearly to the "close friend" it meant nothing of the sort. He saw it as evidence of slackness and lethargy. And his belief, whether justified or not, served to undermine his confidence in Asquith. By contrast, Lloyd George from the outset revealed a prescience regarding the needs of the conflict and readiness to sound a note of stern resolve which equipped him for the role of war leader. Thus, whatever the part Lloyd George played in Asquith's downfall, it was not by intriguing against his chief that he acquired the stature of potential leader of the nation. At best, the "intriguing" was designed to convert potentiality into reality.

What however must be said is that during the war a situation developed in which Asquith required Lloyd George's support to remain in office, and that in ever-increasing degrees that support was withdrawn. Far from attempting to defend his chief against traducers in parliament and the press, Lloyd George identified himself with the position of those who were denouncing Asquith to his advantage. For example, when Simon criticised people who were constantly indulging in "sterile controversies" about the past and "unworthy panic" about the future, and another minister, McKinon Wood, deplored the attitude of pessimists who never looked at what had been done but always at what had not, they were speaking primarily against Asquith's critics in the press. Yet the attitudes they condemned bore a striking resemblance to those publicly adopted by Lloyd George.

Further, Lloyd George never rebuked the newspapers which were denouncing his leader, or said that he would refuse the benefits which they were trying to secure him. His silence did not spring from reluctance to take issue with newspapers. In a speech at Conway on May 6, 1916 he furiously denounced a section of the press, "mischief makers" who should be stamped out and who had discharged "a wave of poison gas" at him. But the newspaper so described was not a right-wing journal campaigning against Asquith; it was the Liberal, pro-Asquith *Daily News,* which had accused Lloyd George of disloyalty to his chief. The manner in which he assailed it made very apparent his failure to criticise Conservative papers which were abusing his leader while sparing him their strictures.

In short, the war having placed Lloyd George in a position to displace Asquith, he did not scruple to seize this opportunity for his advancement. In this respect it is quite beside the point to recall that in December 1916, following Asquith's resignation, he urged Bonar Law to take the premiership. By that time it had become, in part thanks to his activities, too unpleasant a post for anyone but himself to occupy (as well as being a position which large sections of the public and press considered him alone fitted to occupy). Bonar Law had already shown considerable alacrity in abandoning his claim to posts on which Lloyd George had set his heart, like the Ministry of Munitions in May 1915 and the War Office in June 1916. There was no likelihood in December 1916 that the Conservative leader would lay his neck on the chopping-block from which Asquith's head had just rolled. Had Lloyd George really been reluctant to occupy the premiership, he would have shown it during the long period when Asquith was being subjected to unprecedented attacks on his behalf. Far from doing so, he craved for

power so blatantly that he aroused the distrust of nearly all the leading Conservatives. Indeed it required an incipient rebellion of Conservative back-benchers late in 1916 before Bonar Law was finally driven to align with him against Asquith.

As to the merits of Lloyd George's conduct in helping to expel his leader and the main body of Liberals from office, no final judgement is possible. Few will doubt that he was a better war leader than Asquith or that, however dubious his methods, he acted from motives of patriotism as well as self-interest. There seems to have been as much conviction as calculation in his brief, striking appeal to Bonar Law on December 2, 1916, after Asquith had rejected their proposals: "The life of the country depends on resolute action by you now." Yet it still appears that he might have attained effective control of the war without employing the methods he did, had he not been bent on discrediting and replacing, instead of working with, a leader to whom he was profoundly indebted. His contribution to Britain's war effort was outstanding, and yet in the course of it he helped to bring disaster on the Liberal party—a disaster far greater than it need have been had Lloyd George been a man of more scruple and a stronger sense of gratitude.

This is not to say that his ingratitude and lack of scruple were a product of the war. The overweening ambition, the instability of attachment to party and colleagues, and the friendliness towards a type of Conservative least trusted in Liberal circles, were all in evidence before 1914. But hitherto his schemes for a coalition with the Conservatives, and his hankering after an alliance with men like F. E. Smith, had proved abortive and even fanciful. It was the onset of war which made them practicable, and so brought out those facets of his many-sided personality which were to sever his connection with the Liberal party.

Lloyd George was not the only leading Liberal lost to the party at this time. Asquith's attempts to survive politically during the first two years of the war caused him to alienate some of his closest colleagues. This was especially true of Haldane and Churchill. To avoid a Conservative onslaught in May 1915, Asquith agreed to form a coalition in which Haldane was given no office and Churchill so minor an office that he resigned six months later. Both of them deeply resented his failure to stand by them, and neither was to join hands politically with him again. Certainly, Churchill's defection from the Liberal party might have occurred anyway: he was felt to share Lloyd George's political instability and leaning towards the Conservatives, and when war broke out preceded him in urging the formation of a coalition. Nevertheless, his separation from the Liberals was definitely encouraged by Asquith's conduct. And Haldane seems to have been lost principally because of the treatment he received in May 1915. Driven out of politics during the war, he proved ill-disposed thereafter to accept Asquith's overtures to re-enter Liberal politics. Harold Laski found him in 1921 "very Anti-Asquith" on account of the way he had been treated in 1915, and "conducting a twofold flirtation, in part with the Labour party and in part with Lloyd George." In due course the former "flirtation" resulted in his entry into the Labour party and the first Labour government.

The defection of leaders to other parties and political groupings was the clearest manifestation of the way in which the war disintegrated the Liberal leadership. But the party was further weakened by a sharp decline in the reputation of those leaders who remained. Runciman's career was abruptly checked by his failure to cope with shipping problems, Grey's was profoundly injured by misfortunes in his war-time diplomacy, and Augustine Birrell's was shattered beyond repair by the effects of the war on the Irish situation. But the principal casualty, especially in view of his standing in the party and the country, was Asquith himself. When war broke out he was regarded, for all his deficiencies, as a powerful figure adept at resolving differences between ministers, and capable of decisive action in at least some of the crises he encountered. By the end of the war his reputation lay in ruins. He was widely believed to have failed utterly in face of a great challenge, and to have clung to office long after his deficiencies had become apparent. To many who knew him, he seemed by the end of the war a shadow of the leader of old, his grasp and will-power shaken irrevocably by the personal loss he had suffered, the venomous campaign waged against him, the active disloyalty of some of his colleagues, the humiliating retreats to which he had been driven, and the utter finality of his eventual expulsion from office. In a sense Asquith more than anyone reflected the fate of the Liberal party in the war years. Whereas leaders like Lloyd George, Churchill, Haldane, Birrell, Morley, and Burns had by 1918 departed into retirement or fresh political company, Asquith was at least head of the party as he had been in 1914. But with the falling-off in his powers and the air of ineffectiveness and almost non-participation which characterised his conduct, he scarcely resembled the leader who had broken the House of Lords and brought a nation united into war. Far from his retention of the leadership providing a ray of hope for his hard-pressed followers, it seemed almost a further handicap for a party weighed down by difficulties enough.

Trade Union Bid for Supremacy

SAMUEL H. BEER

Labour may have cooperated with the Liberals on the eve of the war, but a decisive break came in 1918. No longer would the Labour parliamentary party consider an electoral association with the Liberals, and it even adopted a socialist program. In the extract below, Samuel H. Beer attributes the end of the old cooperative strategy—and the doom of the Liberals—to increased Labour confidence and a dramatic increase of power for Labour Unions during the war.

W<small>E HAVE YET</small> to ask the question why the Labour party made the decision to adopt Socialism. What is the explanation of this event? If we can identify its causes, we may get some light on the more interesting question of what forces sustained the "orthodoxy" of the Labour Party in succeeding years.

One could begin with the actions and interactions of certain leaders. The principals were Lloyd George and Arthur Henderson. If any one moment is to be singled out as decisive, it surely is the maneuver by which in December, 1916, Asquith was ousted from the premiership and Lloyd George installed in his place. In preparing this coup and in forming his new Government, Lloyd George became deeply beholden to forces that would hardly tolerate in any serious sense "an opening to the Left." His principal supporters in the attack on Asquith, for instance, included Bonar Law, Sir Edward Carson, Max Aitken, and Lord Northcliffe—to mention only a few of the inner core. The new Government, in which the Liberal–Conservative balance shifted sharply toward the Conservatives (fifteen Conservatives received ministerial posts as compared with ten under Asquith), was viewed with deep apprehension by Ernest Bevin, who found in it bitter enemies of the Labour Movement.[1] There was a similar shift to the Right in Lloyd George's majority in Parliament when the Liberals split between Asquith and Lloyd George, who now became heavily dependent upon his Conservative support.

This choice of allies by Lloyd George ultimately led to the breach with Arthur Henderson in August, 1917. In the "doormat incident," Henderson was excluded from a meeting of the Cabinet while it discussed his proposal (which Lloyd George at one time had favored) that British delegates be sent to the proposed International Socialist Congress in Stockholm.[2] His hand probably having been forced by other members of the Cabinet,[3] the Prime Min-

[1] According to Ray Miliband, Bevin complained that "the Cabinet . . . included some of Labour's bitterest enemies." *Parliamentary Socialism* (London, 1961), p. 52. Actually, of the five men Bevin singled out for attack at the party conference of 1917—Lloyd George, Lord Milner, Lord Rhondda, Lord Devonport, and Lord Derby—only the first two were members of the War Cabinet. See 1917 LPCR (*Annual Report of the Labour Party*), pp. 96-7.
[2] David Lloyd George, *War Memoirs* (Boston, 1934), Vol. IV, p. 151.
[3] Henry Pelling, *A Short History of the Labour Party* (London, 1961), p. 41.

From Samuel H. Beer, *Modern British Politics* (London, 1965). Reprinted by permission of Faber and Faber Ltd., and Alfred A. Knopf, pp. 137–140, 144–149.

ister then rejected the Stockholm proposal. With the Labour Party conference fully supporting the proposal, Henderson indignantly resigned from the Government.[4]

Although Labour remained in the Coalition, this incident marked a turning point in the history of the party. In the following months Henderson turned to the dual task of designing a new party organization and framing for the first time a party program. For help in both tasks he enlisted the aid of Sidney Webb, thereby giving to the views of the Fabian Society, which had long been in decline, a major influence on the future of the party. At the conferences of 1918 the party adopted the new constitution and the new program, *Labour and The New Social Order,* with virtually no dissent. "The Labour Party," wrote the American ambassador in January, 1918, "is already playing for supremacy."[5]

An explanation that stopped at this point would leave a great deal unexplained. We can hardly suppose that this major upheaval in the British party system was the result of the decisions and reactions of half a dozen men at the top of British politics. "Right up to 1914," writes Cole, "any attempt to commit the Labour Party to Socialism would have endangered trade union support."[6] Why then were the unions so ready to accept this sharp ideological shift to the Left in 1918? A clue to one possible explanation is given by the speech with which J. H. Thomas initiated the debate on Labour's new program at the conference of June, 1918. During the war, he emphasized, the Government did not entrust the conduct of the economy to private enterprise, but turned to state control. "The taking over of railways, mines and munitions factories and other controlled establishments during the war," he said, "really meant that in the considered judgment of the Government . . . the private ownership of these things in time of war was a danger to the State." In his view it followed that in time of peace private ownership was equally dangerous and state control equally desirable.[7]

This argument, often used by Socialists in the postwar years, rested on the fact that the war effort had involved vast and unprecedented extensions of state power over the economy. These included not only such interferences with the free market as price-fixing and allocation of materials, but also direct government management of the railways and coal mines. As a result of their experience with this wartime system, Stephen Graubard has concluded, "ordinary men and women understood that government control and intervention might mean a larger weekly wage, a more secure employment, and a greater number of social benefits."[8]

One may readily grant that wartime measures taught trade unionists that large-scale state control was practicable as well as beneficial.[9] But to ask for greater state control, even including public ownership of mines and railways, is not the same as to adopt, as Labour did in 1918, the comprehensive ideology of Socialism. For Labour's decision did not consist only in a demand for the particular measures set forth in the program of 1918, multitudinous as they were, but also as I have

---

[4] See M. A. Hamilton, *Arthur Henderson* (London, 1938), p. 155; Stephen Graubard, *British Labour and the Russian Revolution* (Cambridge, Mass., 1956), pp. 23–35; and A. J. P. Taylor's lecture, "Lloyd George, His Rise and Fall" (Cambridge, Eng., 1961).
[5] Quoted in Pelling, *Short History,* p. 42.
[6] *History of the Labour Party from 1914* (London, 1948), p. 53. Ben C. Roberts writes: ". . . it would have been impossible before the war to persuade a majority of the unions that State socialism was a desirable objective." *The Trade Union Congress, 1868–1921* (Cambridge, Mass., 1958), p. 305.

[7] 1918 *LPCR,* p. 43.
[8] "The World War: Labour's Teacher" (unpublished paper delivered before the American Historical Association, 1960).
[9] At the party conference of 1917, G. J. Wardle, who was chairman of the conference as well as chairman of the P.L.P. [Parliamentary Labour Party] and N.E.C. [National Executive Committee], said that the cure for profiteering is "the principles of ownership and control, so long advocated solely by the Labour Party." Referring to government intervention during the war, he then said that "progress in applying [these] principles has been remarkable." 1917 *LPCR,* p. 85.

argued in previous pages, in a commitment to a new system, a "new social order," indeed a "new civilisation." This ideological break with Liberalism was intimately related to the other major decision, the adoption of a new framework of organization.

*   *   *

The crucial shift in union opinion took place during the war. This cannot be traced to a sharp deterioration in the material condition of the working class. On the contrary, it can be argued that as a whole the working class was materially better off during the war than before.[10] The most striking correlation, in actual fact, is with the immense rise in trade union membership since 1914. Henderson could respond aggressively to the "doormat incident" not only because the Liberals were split, but also because the growth of trade unionism at last provided the party with the means for a strategy of full-fledged independence. Moreover, the increase in organizational power of the unions did more than merely provide an opportunity for this strategy. It also virtually forced the Labour Party to adopt it and to break politically with the Liberals. The commitment to Socialism, in turn, can be regarded as a consequence of this breach. In other words, the adoption of the new ideology was not so much a cause as an effect of the hardly avoidable break with the Liberals.[11] Underlying this

rupture were the divisive forces of the British class structure at the time.

The basic dynamic factor was the growth in trade union membership. Membership in unions affiliated with the T.U.C., one must recall, had grown very slowly in the past. By 1900, thirty-two years after the founding of the Congress, it had reached 1,250,000. By 1913 it had risen to only 2,232,446. Then with the war came a sudden and dramatic upsurge, in five years membership doubled, reaching 4,532,985 in 1918, the trend continuing upward to 6,505,482 in 1920.[12] Membership in the Labour Party had followed a roughly parallel course. From 375,931 in 1900, it had risen to just short of 1,000,000 in 1906 and stood at 1,612,147 in 1914. Then, nearly doubling, it reached 3,013,129 in 1918 and rose in the next two years to 4,359,807. Similarly, the local organization of the party grew hardly at all before the war. In 1908 there were 134 local bodies, either local associations or trades councils. By 1914 these had grown to only 158. As compared with this net increase of only 24 in six years, the number of local bodies grew by 102 between 1914 and 1917, reaching a total of 260 in the latter year.[13] This, it should be observed, was before the great increase in local bodies that resulted from the new form of organization adopted in 1918.[14]

In short, as these figures show, the great growth in trade union membership was a necessary condition for the growth of the Labour Party which, its strength more efficiently mobilized by the new constitution, was able to field 361 candidates in the General Election of 1918, as compared

---

[10] Although the cost of living rose faster than wages (Ben C. Roberts, op. cit., p. 287), on the other hand, an immense amount of overtime was worked and many wives and daughters of working class households entered industry. As a result, one historian is prompted to write, there was "a very marked rise in the standard of living throughout the wage-earning classes." "Organized labour," he continues, "was determined that these standards should be maintained after the war." D. C. Somervell, British Politics Since 1900 (London, 1950), p. 108.
[11] Henderson explicitly reasoned along these lines, judging by G. D. H. Cole's reconstruction of his intentions. Cole writes: "His [.ie., Henderson's] study of the position had, however, convinced him, by 1917, that some sort of Socialist faith was the necessary basis for the consolidation of the Labour Party into an effective national force." Henderson, continues Cole, "turned naturally" to

Fabian Socialism for "the new gospel which he needed to give substance to the Constitution that he had in mind." Op. cit., p. 60.

[12] Ben C. Roberts, The Trade Union Congress, 1886–1921 (Cambridge, Mass., 1958), p. 309.
[13] G. D. H. Cole, British Working Class Politics 1832–1914 (London, 1941) p. 50.
[14] In 1918, under the new constitution, the number of local bodies rose to 398, of which 73 were trades councils and 325 political. Cole, op. cit., p. 50.

with only 78 and 56 in the two elections of 1910. The results of the election of 1918 tell the same story of a major advance, constituting a qualitative change in the power position of the movement. Although the number of Labour M.P.'s returned was only 60, the total vote for Labour relative to that of other parties showed an immense increase. The percentage of total vote won by the Labour Party had shown only slight gains before the war: 5.4 in 1906, 8.1 in 1910 (January), and 7.7 in 1910 (December). Then, in the 1918 election, it rose to 23.9, continuing upward to reach 30.0 in 1922, when the party became the leading Opposition party in Parliament.

The *entente* with the Liberals, explicit in 1906 and tacit in 1910, had depended upon Labour's ability to put forward only a modest number of candidates. How could this relationship have been maintained when the immense growth in trade unionism meant that the party would present not a few score, but several hundred candidates? How could Labour have avoided a broad nationwide electoral challenge to the Liberals? One possibility would have been for the Liberals to have refrained from putting up candidates in scores, even hundreds of constituencies, in the expectation that Liberal voters would support the Labour candidate. Labour presumably would have done the same in some equivalent number of cases. But can one conceive of the middle and upper class personnel of the local Liberal associations abdicating in this manner and on such a scale in favor of working-class candidates? And if they had, the effect would have been not so much cooperation as fusion. Nominally, of course, the possibility of fusion was open under the formal organization of the local Liberal parties. Theoretically, trade unionists could have joined and, where they won a majority, have nominated whoever they pleased for Parliament. But in practice, as previous experience had shown, the middle- and upper-class leaders of the local caucuses would resist any such implementation, however logical, of the theory of Radical

democracy on which presumably their extra-parliamentary organization was founded.

These speculations are merely intended to direct attention to the fundamental and hardly obscure fact that in Edwardian and post-Edwardian Britain class antagonism drew a bold line through British politics. "In the world of Edwardian England," Alan Bullock writes, "an impassable gulf still separated the man in a cloth cap from the classes born and educated to conduct the affairs of State."[15] The middle- and upper-class leaders of local Liberal associations were happy to cultivate the votes of the working class. They would have them as members of the caucus so long as they did not try to assert a claim to leadership. They were even ready to go far toward recognizing the "interests of labour," as was shown when Liberal Councils welcomed measures of social reform introduced by their Governments at the instigation of Labour. They refused, however, to share their power.

This refusal goes back to the days of Lib–Lab politics. Hardie, MacDonald, and Henderson had all personally experienced it. The decline of the Labour Electoral Association resulted from its inability to get Liberal caucuses to adopt working-class (i.e., trade unionist) candidates, a failure that turned the thoughts of many labor leaders toward a separate party. Moreover, the *entente* established between the two parties by MacDonald and Gladstone was severely limited in scope and time. It depended, as we have seen, on the weakness of the Labour Party. It lasted, even in a tacit and attenuated form, only through the elections of 1910. Thereafter, as Cole has observed, the Liberal associations were not prepared to allow Labour men any further seats; indeed, they were disposed to reclaim seats which had been held by Lib–Labs. On the eve of the war, collabo-

[15] *The Life and Times of Ernest Bevin*, Vol. I, p. 27.

ration in the constituencies had virtually ceased to exist.[16]

This refusal by local Liberals to accept greater representation for the organized working class either by means of Lib–Lab or outright Labour candidates was recognized and lamented by some Liberal leaders.[17] But they themselves made no great effort to bring Labour men into the inner circle of power. Apart from John Burns—and by 1906 his ties with organized labor were tenuous—no trade unionist was given ministerial office before the war and only minor posts were offered Shackleton and other trade union officials.[18] The Liberal leaders in Westminster were no more willing to share power at their level than the local Liberals were at theirs.

Trade unionists had good reason to regard the caucus as "a middle class machine."[19] But one should not neglect the independent force of the demand among the organized working class for a political instrument of their own. They too were class conscious, and did not merely react to the middle-class rebuff; they also were increasing, as trade unionism grew, their demand for political power as a class. Some remarks of Ernest Bevin's to a group of employers during the war reflect these sentiments. The subject was industrial relations, not politics, but Bevin's rugged language gave voice to this strong sense of separateness in identity and destiny:

I had to work at ten years of age while my employer's son went to the university until he was twenty. You have set out for me a different set of conditions. I was taught to bow to the squire and touch my hat to the parson; my employer's son was not. All these things have produced within me an intense hatred, a hatred which has caused me to organise for my fellows and direct my mind to a policy to give to my class a power to control their own destiny and labour.

. . . At present employers and employed are, too often, separated by something akin to a barrier of "caste." . . . The operatives are frequently regarded by employers as being of a different and inferior order. . . . So long as these views continue to exist they inevitably produce an intense class bitterness.[20]

In Edwardian and post-Edwardian Britain there was the normal clash of interest between employers and employees. But one may doubt whether this clash alone would have sufficed to maintain the divorce between Liberals and trade unionists. After all, even when trade unionists had accepted Gladstonian economics, they found it impossible to win a place of equality in the Liberal Party. Throughout the generation before 1918, whether wages were high or low, the unions gaining or losing, government favorable or unfavorable, the nation at war or at peace, the strong sense of class —on both sides—powerfully reinforced the clash of interest, preventing any unity closer than a transient and limited collaboration. Given such a division of sentiments, it is hard to see how the powerful trade union movement, having reached the heights of power that it occupied in 1918, could have failed to break definitively with the Liberals and make its separate bid for political supremacy.

The adoption of Socialism as an ideology was functional to this choice of political independence. If the party was to pursue power independently, it needed a set of beliefs and values distinguishing it from other parties. For the sake of its own

---

[16] Cole, *op. cit.*, p. 224.
[17] In 1892 Herbert Gladstone admitted, "The long and short of it is that the constituencies, for social, financial and trade reasons are extremely slow to adopt Labour candidates." Quoted in Pelling, *The Origins of the Labour Party 1880–1900* (London, 1954), p. 237. In 1901 Gladstone, by now Liberal Chief Whip, wrote: "I could come to terms with the leaders of the Labour party. . . . The difficulty lies with the constituencies . . . and the unfortunate necessity of providing funds." Quoted in Bealey and Pelling, *Labour and Politics 1900–1906: A History of the Labour Representation Committee* (London, 1958), p. 131.
[18] Roberts, *op. cit.*, p. 242.
[19] So characterized by Threlfall, the leader of the Labour Electoral Association, in 1894. Pelling, *Origins of the Labour Party*, p. 236.

[20] Quoted in Bullock, *op. cit.*, Vol. I, pp. 69 and 70.

followers, present and prospective, the party had to articulate in its declaration of purpose the profound sense of difference—or if you like, alienation—that sprang from their consciousness of class. In 1918 there still were, to be sure, a few labor leaders who favored not a Socialist, but only a "trade union" party. Such a party championing traditional union interests and some broader social reforms might have been viable. But such a party purpose and program would have retained strong ideological links with the Radical wing of the Liberal Party. In the constituencies it would have made a sharp electoral challenge to the Liberals far more difficult. It could never have provided, as Socialism did, the intellectual basis for the missionary zeal that party activists displayed in the years ahead. One can only agree with the wisdom of Arthur Henderson when he concluded in 1917 that "some sort of Socialist faith was the necessary basis for the consolidation of the Labour Party into an effective national force."[21]

[21] Cole, *History of the Labour Party*, p. 60.

The Decision of Lloyd George

ROY JENKINS

Roy Jenkins has successfully combined the practice of politics and the
writing of political history. First taking a seat in the House of Commons in
1948 as a Labour member, he has held important cabinet positions in the
Labour government of 1964. He has also written several excellent biographies
and political studies, including *Mr. Attlee: An Interim Biography* (1948), *Mr.
Balfour's Poodle* (1954), *Sir Charles Dilke: A Victorian Tragedy* (1958), and
Asquith (1964). Jenkins maintains that the displacement of Asquith in 1916
left much bitterness but did not make the party split irreparable. It was
decisions of Lloyd George in 1918, he says, which made the division permanent, and thereby the destruction of the Liberal party certain.

ASQUITH spent his first Christmas
out of office in the Isle of Wight,
at a house lent by his former War Minister, Seely, and then saw in the New
Year of 1917 at the Wharf, with Margot
and "a few intimates." This was close to
the pattern of any of the preceding six
years, but there was no familiar press of
events as soon as the holidays were over.
"It is a novel sensation for me to be master
of my own time all day long," he wrote on
January 2nd.

He was neither bored nor unoccupied.
His intellectual resources were too manifold for that. He had been reading "*Shakespeare's England* and Stow's *Survey of
London* with some dips into Heraldry and
browsing in *The Ship of Fooles*—written
by an old monk called Barclay just on the
eve of the Reformation." But, more than
most Prime Ministers who have just ceased
to hold office, he had no clear political role.
He had not retired: he did not feel ready
for this, and he was still head of the Liberal Party. As such he was nominally leader
of the opposition. When the House of
Commons met again, he sat opposite the
left-hand despatch box, asked the business

occasions. But who comprised the opposition, and where did Asquith want to lead
them?

There was no doubt about the former
questions, and spoke second on ceremonial
Liberal ministers who sat alongside him on
the front bench. Some of them were much
more aggressively disposed to the new Government than he was himself. The attitude
of the Liberal back-benchers was less clear.
Although they had given Asquith his
unanimous vote of confidence at the
National Liberal Club meeting, at least
126 of them, according to Christopher
Addison, one of Lloyd George's few Liberal ministers, had agreed to support the
new Coalition. Asquith himself did not
intend to oppose it. It never for a moment
occurred to him that Lloyd George, having obtained power, could or should be
overturned without the opportunity to give
his new system of government a run for
its money. The country was in the midst
of a desperate struggle. Political activity in
the constituencies, largely by Asquith's
own wish, was at a standstill. In these circumstances any normal opposition role
would have been both dangerous and

From Roy Jenkins, *Asquith* (London, 1964). Reprinted by permission of Collins Publishers and Chil-
mark Press, pp. 464-465, 467.

84

ineffective. It would also have been distasteful to Asquith. He interpreted his commitment to help keep opinion steady and frustrate the spread of opposition to the war in much more than a purely formal way. He felt a heavy, continuing responsibility for the decision of August 4th, 1914, and he was genuinely nervous of damaging national unity.

Even had he felt otherwise, he would at this stage have found little room for manoeuvre. His motives would have been too open to misinterpretation. The charge of personal jealousy would have been raised against him, with the newspapers ensuring that it echoed around the country with the utmost shrillness. The Press lords remained curiously unappeased by his fall. They showed no magnanimity in victory, and continued to lay the blame for anything that went wrong at his door. As a result, the danger was, not that Asquith might be tempted to be too hostile to the new Government, but that his utility as even a gently probing critic was seriously undermined. Ironically, the only other Prime Minister of the century who, leaving office with his physical powers unimpaired, was to find himself equally bereft of a role, was Lloyd George. The process of Liberal self-destruction had begun.

*　*　*

During the remainder of 1917 and early 1918 Asquith kept up a moderate level of political activity. He paid a visit to the Western Front as the guest of Haig. He maintained contact with the leaders of the Irish party. He spoke quite often in the House of Commons. He declared his support, fatalistically for women's suffrage, far-sightedly for proportional representation, and enthusiastically for President Wilson's idea of a League of Nations. He made occasional speeches in the country, at Liverpool in October, 1917, at Birmingham two months later, and at Manchester in September, 1918. He delivered a carefully-prepared and widely circulated Romanes lecture at Oxford entitled *On the Victorian Age*. But, until the late spring of 1918, he delivered no challenge to the Government. His speeches were cautious, and he never entered the division lobby against Lloyd George.

Then came the Maurice debate. On May 7th, Major-General Sir Frederick Maurice wrote a letter to several newspapers. Maurice, the son of Charles Kingsley's Christian Socialist friend and the father of the economist Joan Robinson, was not a typical soldier. His letter contained a series of challenges to the accuracy of ministerial statements. The most important of these was directed at the Prime Minister. The military background to the challenge was that the Germans, during March and April, had launched two sledgehammer blows—the first instalments of their all-out drive for victory before the Americans arrived—against the British sector of the Western Front. Both the attacks were eventually contained, but not before the biggest advances since 1914 had been made, Amiens and Hazebrouck had been threatened, and morale at home had been badly shaken. In addition, another staggering wave of casualties had been suffered, and Haig had been driven to the limit of his reserves. But why were his reserves so low? Why were some of his divisions "skeletonised" even before the attacks began?

The suspicion was that Lloyd George, as a counter to Haig's fondness for bloody offensives (Passchendaele had been the culmination of the previous autumn's slaughter) deliberately kept him short of troops. The Commander-in-Chief, according to the Prime Minister's plan, would have to save casualties by remaining on the defensive throughout 1918. In the outcome, however, the plan had greatly increased them, and nearly lost the war as well. This was the result of Lloyd George's upstart conviction that he knew better than the soldiers. So, at least, some of the criticism ran. Lloyd George replied by denying the premiss. "Notwithstanding the heavy casualties in 1917," he told the House of Commons on April 9th, "the army in France was considerably stronger on 1st January, 1918, than on 1st January, 1917."

General Maurice, who was Director of Military Operations at the War Office until late April (when he was removed by the C.I.G.S. Sir Henry Wilson), wrote to denounce this statement. "(It) implies," he said, "that Sir Douglas Haig's fighting strength of the eve of the great battle which began on 21st March had not been diminished. That is not correct." He also denied the accuracy of a statement by Bonar Law about the circumstances in which a recent extension of the British line had been agreed upon, and of another by the Prime Minister relating to troop strength in the Middle East. He referred to Law's statement as "the latest of a series of mis-statements which have been made recently in the House of Commons by the present Government." He used the phrase "that is not correct" as a reiterative chorus after each of Lloyd George's claims. He passed to a justification of his own action. The falseness of these statements was appreciated by a large number of soldiers and "this knowledge is breeding such distrust of the Government as can only end by impairing the splendid morale of our troops."

"I have therefore decided," he ended, "fully realising the consequences to myself, that my duty as a citizen must over-ride my duty as a soldier, and I ask you to publish this letter, in the hope that Parliament may see fit to order an investigation into the statements I have made."

The letter was a heavy challenge to the Government. It was also a clear breach of military discipline, as Maurice himself admitted by implication. But was it in addition, as Lloyd George insisted in his *War Memoirs,* part of a general Asquithian plot "to blow up the Government?" The evidence is against this. Maurice was well-known to Asquith, who held him in high regard, and the general no doubt looked to the former Prime Minister to press the matter in Parliament. But he had not consulted him beforehand, although he had very nearly done so. The first that Asquith heard was when he received the following letter from Maurice on the morning of publication:

> 20, Kensington Park Gardens,
> 6. 5. 1918

Dear Mr. Asquith,

I have today sent to the press a letter which will, I hope, appear in tomorrow's papers. When I asked you to see me last Thursday, I had intended to consult you about this letter, but on second thoughts I came to the conclusion that, if I consulted you, it would be tantamount to asking you to take responsibility for the letter, and that I alone must take that responsibility. I ask you to believe that in writing the letter I have been guided solely by what I hold to be the public interest.

> Believe me,
> Yours sincerely,
> F. Maurice

Even without prior consultation, Asquith acted rapidly. That afternoon he asked a private notice question of Bonar Law (as leader of the House). Law replied that the Government proposed to ask two judges to act as "a court of honor" and to enquire into the alleged mis-statements. During supplementary questions the idea of a judicial enquiry came under heavy fire, and not only from Asquith. Another Liberal, George Lambert, first put forward the alternative demand for a select committee of the House of Commons. Carson, who had once again resigned from the Government, made several menacing interventions about the need for Cabinet and (perhaps more significantly) ex-Cabinet ministers to be absolved from their oaths of secrecy when appearing before the enquiry. Asquith demanded a debate before a decision. Law countered by offering to let Asquith nominate the two judges. Asquith refused to be mollified by this and persisted in his demand that the issue must be debated before the court of enquiry was set up.

As soon as he left the chamber Bonar

Law found that his offer was as ill-received by some of his colleagues in the Government as by the Asquithians and Carson. Churchill argued vehemently against a judicial enquiry on grounds of high principle, and carried the Prime Minister with him. A minister, he said, should never ask judges to enquire into his own integrity. In view of this sudden movement of opinion it was fortunate for the Government that Asquith had not immediately accepted Law's offer.

The debate came on two days later. Asquith moved that a select committee of the House of Commons be set up. His speech was brief and restrained, but uncertain and therefore unconvincing in tone. He disclaimed any desire to censure the Government. He had believed that they might accept his motion. Drawing with some effect upon his experience of the Parnell Commission, he pronounced against the method of judicial enquiry. But when an interrupter suggested that the Marconi select committee provided an equally unsatisfactory precedent for this method, he returned no adequate answer. He was also put out when he asked the rhetorical question: "What is the alternative (to the select committee)?" and received from a somewhat jingoistic miners' member, the reply of "Get on with the war."

At the conclusion of his speech Asquith drew from Bonar Law the typically stark argument that a select committee could never be impartial because there was no member of the House who was not "either friendly (to) or opposed to the Government." After expressing his dismay at hearing such unparliamentary statements from the leader of the House, but without any attempt to weave his own points into a final crescendo of argument, Asquith sat down. There was no sense of a great parliamentary occasion about his speech. He had chosen a minor key, and had played it without his usual sureness of touch.

Lloyd George, who followed, struck a different note. He spoke for 1¼ hours, nearly twice as long as Asquith, but the pace of his speech was much faster. He was determined to escape from the judicial enquiry offer, to force the issue there and then, to refute and discredit Maurice, to accuse Asquith of having been party to a fractious plot to bring down the Government, and to secure an overwhelming vote of vindication from the House of Commons. He succeeded in all these objectives. He not only destroyed the demand for a select committee. He also laid down the principle, which prevailed for the rest of the war, that House of Commons criticism of the Government's military leadership was equivalent to disloyal sabotage of the national effort. His speech was a great parliamentary *tour de force*.

Asquith felt the force of the storm, but did not bow before it. Wisely or unwisely, he had committed himself to put down his motion and, if necessary, to vote for it. He had argued the case on purely procedural grounds, whereas Lloyd George had insisted, with daring persuasiveness, in bringing the substance of the matter before the House. This unbalanced the debate from the beginning, and the critics of the Government never recovered their equilibrium. But Asquith did not feel that he could be driven into withdrawal by Lloyd George's aggressive tactics. He watched passively the unsatisfactory unfolding of the debate. It lasted less than three hours after the Prime Minister sat down. Carson turned about and gave almost wholehearted support to Lloyd George. Three Conservatives —General Croft, Colonel Archer-Shee and Lord Hugh Cecil—delivered damaging criticisms of the Government, Croft in particular applying himself to the substance of the dispute, and said they would abstain. Joynson-Hicks and two others, one a Liberal and one a Conservative, said that they had come with open minds, but had been convinced by the Prime Minister that there was no case for an enquiry. Colonel

Josiah Wedgwood said that he had three times changed his mind as to how to vote, and appealed despairingly for some further guidance from the front opposition bench.

He appealed in vain. McKenna was there, Runciman was there, Samuel was there. But none of them rose to wind up. The debate petered out, with brief inconclusive speeches and increasingly impatient shouts of "divide, divide." Asquith mustered a vote of 108 (including the two tellers), made up of 100 Liberals and a minority of the Labour members. The Government had 295, including 71 Liberals. Asquith and his followers went gloomily home. They could not have been pleased with themselves. They had been badly out-manoeuvred. But they had no idea that they had participated in one of the great divisive debates of history, in an event from which Lloyd George would never allow the Liberal Party to recover.

What were the merits of the argument? Did Asquith eagerly seize upon the false accusations of a sour and neurotic general (as Lloyd George insisted on regarding Maurice) or did the Prime Minister tear up the truth in order to discomfort his critics and gain a spurious House of Commons victory? Lloyd George, in his speech, rested upon two sets of alternative defences. The first was that his statements were correct, but that, even if they were not, the responsibility was Maurice's who, as Director of Military Operations, had supplied him with the figures. The second was that, in making his comparison between January, 1917 and January, 1918 he had not included the non-combatant troops (labour battalions etc.), which had grown greatly in strength in the interval, but that he would in fact have been justified in doing so, as the distinction was an unreal one.

The last point would have been a difficult one to sustain in detailed argument, and in any event it had been discounted in a parliamentary answer by the under-secretary for War on April 18th. So far as combatant troops were concerned, however, the final War Office (pre-debate) figures did not bear out Lloyd George's contention. Those prepared on May 7th gave a total of 1,198,032 in January, 1918, as compared with 1,283,696 in January, 1917. Yet Lloyd George had acted in good faith and on War Office authority when he made his statement on April 9th; and Maurice was directly involved in providing that authority.

How, then, did the discrepancy arise? Part of the explanation was provided four years later. General Maurice, seeking to vindicate himself, and after a careful review of the facts, wrote to Lloyd George in July, 1922. The War Office document upon which Lloyd George's first statements was based, he said, had been prepared in a hurry. By mistake the strength of the armies in Italy had been included in those in France. This mistake was quickly discovered, however (so one would hope, for the sake of General Maurice's reputation as head of the Military Operations department), and a correction was sent to Lloyd George within a few days. When the Prime Minister made his May 9th statement, therefore, he did so on the basis of information which he knew had since been amended.

But did he? In 1922 he brushed Maurice's letter aside. He was never a man for the careful unravelling of past mysteries, particularly if the process might be embarrassing to him. He preferred the events of the moment, and he wanted no dealings with Maurice. At this stage, therefore, the matter remained unresolved. But in 1934 Lady Lloyd George (then Miss Frances Stevenson and still, as she had been for many years, one of Lloyd George's most trusted secretaries) made an entry in her diary. And in 1956 Lord Beaverbrook, making use of his vast store of early twentieth century political papers, revealed this entry. It ran as follows:

Have been reading up the events connected with the Maurice Debate in order to help Ll.G. with this chapter in volume v (of the *War*

Memoirs), and am uneasy in my mind about an incident which occurred at the time and is known only to J. T. Davies[1] and myself. Ll.G. obtained from the W.O. the figures which he used in his statement on April 9th in the House of Commons on the subject of manpower. These figures were afterwards stated by Gen. Maurice to be incorrect.

I was in J. T. Davies' room a few days after the statement, and J.T. was sorting out red despatch boxes to be returned to the Departments. As was his wont he looked in them before locking them up and sending them out to the Messengers. Pulling out a W.O. box, he found in it, to his great astonishment, a paper from the D.M.O. containing modifications and corrections of the first figures they had sent, and by some mischance this box had remained unopened. J.T. and I examined it in dismay, and then J.T. put it in the fire, remarking, "Only you and I, Frances, know of the existence of this paper."

There is no doubt that this is what Maurice had in mind when he accused Ll.G. of misstatement. But the amazing thing was that *the document was never fixed upon.* . . . I was waiting for the matter to be raised, and for the question to be asked: Why did L.G. not receive these supplementary figures? Or did he? But the question never came and I could not voluntarily break faith with J.T., perhaps put L.G. in a fix, and who knows, have brought down the Government!

I suppose it is too late for the matter to be cleared up and I had better keep silent. But I will talk it over with J.T. In any event, no good could come of any revelation made now. . . .

So, with this interesting sidelight on Downing Street life under the Lloyd George régime, the mystery appears to be cleared up. So far at least as his main charge was concerned, Maurice was right. Asquith knew that he was right, and acted from a high sense of duty, although with less than his usual parliamentary skill. But Lloyd George may genuinely have believed that Maurice, saying one thing in

[1] Sir J. T. Davies, 1881–1938, Lloyd George's principal private secretary from 1912 until the end of his premiership. Subsequently a director of the Suez Canal Company and a trustee of the Lloyd George Fund.

the War Office and another as soon as he was outside, was a conspirator against the Government rather than a performer of public duty. Nor did the Prime Minister understand how he had been misled on April 9th. He can therefore be acquitted of the heaviest charges which are laid against his conduct of the Maurice debate. The use which he subsequently made of it is a different matter.

This use occurred seven months later. During the first half of 1918 the end of the war seemed almost infinitely remote. The generals and the politicians were thinking in terms of the campaigns of 1919 and 1920. And the public, which in 1914–15 had found it so difficult to adjust to the idea of a long war, now found it almost equally difficult to comprehend that peace might be near at hand. By the early autumn, however, the mood had changed. Asquith, who had spent a quite summer, golfing at North Berwick and (a most uncharacteristic activity) climbing "on about the hottest afternoon of the year" to the highest of the Clumps behind Sutton Courtney, was deeply embroiled, by early October, in talks about the peace prospect and the possible terms. "I came up here yesterday morning," he wrote from Cavendish Square on October 8th, "a day sooner than I intended, as I wanted to be in touch with people about this German Peace Note . . . Lansdowne and Gilbert Murray are coming to lunch: E. Grey after lunch: and Lord Reading about tea-time: so I am not wanting for counsellors."

Asquith believed at this stage that he might have a great part to play in the peace negotiations, and in the subsequent reconstruction of Europe. He had a good deal of traditional English scepticism about the intentions and capacity of the Americans, but he was most anxious to meet Woodrow Wilson and to co-operate closely with him. When he heard that the President was coming to London he wrote:

I confess he is one of the few people in the world that I want to see and talk to: not quite in the spirit of Monckton Milnes, of whom it was said that if Christ came again he would at once send him an invitation card for one of his breakfasts; but because I am really curious to judge for myself what manner of man he is. Gilbert Murray, who was here this morning and knows him, thinks that I should like him.

Asquith's assumption was still that the Liberal Party would retain a dominant position in post-war politics. The process of disillusionment began, mildly at first, in early November. Lloyd George, following up a series of October talks, had written a formal but for the moment secret letter to Bonar Law on November 2nd, proposing that there should be a quick election and a Coalition ticket. Ten days later this proposal was accepted at a Unionist meeting. Before that Asquith had gathered what was intended. "I suppose that tomorrow we shall be told the final decision about this accursed General Election," he wrote on November 6th. "If, as seems more than likely, it is to be upon us soon after the end of the month, it will be difficult to make any plans, as one may find oneself roaming about like the Wandering Jew." A strong deputation from Liberals in the constituencies waited upon Lloyd George during this week and urged him to fight in alliance, not with Bonar Law, but with Asquith. They received a discouraging answer. Asquith was of course informed of what occurred at this meeting.

Then came the Armistice. Asquith had only a peripheral part to play in that dramatic and emotion-charged day of brilliant autumn sunlight. His main duty during the morning was to motor to Golders Green and attend the cremation service of a distant relation. When he returned he found a telegram from the King (in reply to one which Margot had sent earlier in their joint names). "I look back with gratitude," it said, "to your wise counsel and calm resolve in the days when great issues had to be decided resulting in our entry into the war." After luncheon he drove with Margot to the House of Commons, and listened to Lloyd George reading the terms of the Armistice. He contributed a few brief but appropriate remarks. The House then adjourned and moved in procession to St. Margaret's for a service of thanksgiving. At Cavendish Square Margot had ordered all available flags to be put out, and Asquith found a Welsh harp "fluttering greenly" from his library window. The next day the Asquiths attended the national thanksgiving service at St. Paul's, and lunched afterwards with the King and Queen at Buckingham Palace.

Sometime in the next few days Asquith had an important interview with Lloyd George. Although at least three accounts of this survive, none of them fixes the day, but it seems likely to have been in the week following the Armistice. None of these accounts is in serious conflict with another, so perhaps Margot's version (always the most graphic) may be given:

. . . Henry was asked to go to the Prime Minister's room in the House of Commons.

Upon his return he told me what had occurred. He had been received with a friendliness which amounted to enthusiasm and asked where he stood. Mr. Lloyd George then said:

"I understand you don't wish to take a post under the Government."

To which my husband answered that that was so; and added that the only service he thought he could render the Government would be if he were to go to Versailles, as from what he knew both of President Wilson and M. Clemenceau he was pretty sure they knew little of International Law or finance, and that these two problems would be found all-important in view of fixing future frontiers and the havoc the war was likely to create in all the Foreign Exchanges.

At this Mr. Lloyd George looked a little confused. He was walking up and down the room, and in knocking up against a chair a pile of loose books were thrown upon the ground. Hastily looking at his watch and stooping down to pick up the books, he said he would consider my husband's proposal. Nothing more was said; the interview was over, and my husband never heard another word upon the matter.

Neither of the two was willing to accept the other's terms. Asquith was loath either to compromise his position as the head of an independent Liberal Party, or to desert his old friends, by entering the Coalition Government. Lloyd George was determined that, if Asquith wanted to go to Paris, he should first pay the price of subordinating himself in the Government. The *impasse* was complete, although Asquith continued to hope, even when the election had left its legacy of additional bitterness that he might still be allowed his independent delegate status.

The election campaign was as disagreeable for the independent Liberals as it was discreditable for the leaders of the Coalition. Lloyd George unaccountably claimed that he did not allude to the Maurice debate "during the whole contest," but in fact he raised it at length (although without mentioning the name "Maurice") at one of the first meetings—Wolverhampton on November 23rd—and made it clear that performance the previous May was to be the principal test of whether or not a sitting Liberal M.P. was to receive the endorsement of Bonar Law and himself. Nearly all who had voted for the select committee were provided with Coalition opponents—mostly Unionists. In this way "the coupon," as Asquith described it, was born.

Asquith fought a campaign of integrity, but a slightly weary and dispirited one. "I doubt whether so far there is much interest in the elections," he wrote on November 25th, "despite the efforts of the newspapers to keep the pot boiling. The whole thing is a wicked fraud, which will settle nothing." And on another occasion: "I am rather in need of something to read on my journeys: I loathe all this knocking about, but it has to be done."

He had some good meetings and found the Liberals on occasion "breast-high against all this coalitioneering." But it would be an exaggeration to say that he was optimistic about the general result. The best that he could hope for was to maintain a bastion of a hundred or so independent Liberal seats against the Coalition flood. Most of these, he believed, would hold. In particular, he felt no doubts about East Fife. "I confess that I felt so little apprehension for my seat that I spent most of my time . . . in visiting and addressing other constituencies," he wrote. He was there for polling day, however, and was edified by posters somewhat clumsily proclaiming: "Asquith nearly lost you the War. Are you going to let him spoil the Peace?"

The results were delayed for a fortnight to allow the soldiers' votes to come in. This interval included Christmas, and Asquith spent most of it at the Wharf. He did not return to Scotland for the counting. That day (December 28th) he began by leading a deputation of Grey and Gilbert Murray to tell President Wilson of their support for the idea of the League of Nations. Later in the morning he went to see the Freedom of the City of London conferred upon the President. The freedom ceremony over, the company adjourned to the Mansion House for a Lord Mayor's luncheon. Asquith sat at the high table, only a few places away from Lloyd George. As the meal drew to an end whispers of the election returns began to circulate amongst the guests. On their way out the air was heavy with fact and rumour. It was clear that the Coalition had won a crushing victory. Margot described the scene:

. . . I heard a man say: "Herbert Samuel, McKinnon Wood and Runciman are out."

We left the dining-room and made our way down to the crowded front door. People waiting for their motors were standing in groups discussing the Election returns.

"McKenna is beat: Montagu is in by over 9,000" was whispered from mouth to mouth, while the men thrust their arms into their coat sleeves, changing their cigars from hand to hand in the process, and asking for their motors.

The news spread; man after man of ours was out.

Were we all *beaten*? . . . . Who *could* I ask? Who would tell me? Henry crushed up against me and said calmly:

"I see our footman" . . .

Among the crush in the large open doorway . . . I perceived Rufus Reading, looking snow-white. Did he or did he not know if Henry was beaten? . . . perhaps they all knew.

I was jammed up against my husband and had no idea what he had heard.

I looked at him out of the corner of my eye-lids; he was standing a little in front of me, but not a sign of any kind could be seen on his face. . . .

I saw as if in a trance the cheering crowds, eager faces, mounted police, and swaying people, while we shot down the streets with our minds set and stunned. Not one word did we say till we got near home; then Henry broke the silence:

"I only hope," he said, "that *I* have not got in; with all the others out this would be the last straw."

. . . The motor slowed down; we had arrived. I jumped out and ran through the open door in front of Henry; I found the odd man labelling our luggage piled up in the hall. Not a note or a message of any kind was to be seen.

Henry went into his library, and I rang up 21 Abingdon Street (the Liberal headquarters) on the telephone in my boudoir.

"Not got all the returns? . . . Yes? . . . East Fife. Yes? . . . Asquith beat? . . . Thank God . . ."

Henry came in . . .

"I'm out, am I?" he said; "ask by how much; tell them to give us the figures, will you?"

"Give me the East Fife figures," I said, and taking a pencil wrote:

Asquith 6994—Sprott 8996.

The blow was of course a crippling one. However much both he and Margot might bravely protest that, with nearly all the others out, it was better for Asquith to be beaten too, this was not so. It spared him the early years of a harsh and hostile Parliament, but at the price of a personal humiliation which destroyed his hope of exercising any influence on the peace settlement. He was the rejected man, whose constituency of thirty-two years' standing had not even needed the spur of the coupon (Lloyd George and Bonar Law, with self-conscious generosity, had withheld it from the Conservative Sprott) to vote him out. The wheel of political fortune had indeed turned full circle for him. After three decades of mounting success almost all power had crumbled away in two years. He was left with only a remnant of a party, and no forum from which to lead it.

Incompetence and Selfishness of Asquith

A. J. P. TAYLOR

A. J. P. Taylor, Fellow of Magdalen College, Oxford, is one of England's leading and most controversial historians. Each of his many studies in nineteenth and twentieth century European history has raised a storm of comment. His supporters find him brilliantly stimulating, and his critics see him as brilliantly irresponsible. Even his keenest detractors, however, admit that his volume on twentieth-century England is a worthy addition to the celebrated *Oxford History of England* series. In the selection given here Taylor displays his usual verve and wit—and his willingness to make sharp judgments. His treatment of Lloyd George's rise to power should be compared with the extracts from Trevor Wilson and Roy Jenkins.

WAR SOCIALISM or a negotiated peace [in 1916] were the stark alternatives over which men would have disputed if they had been conscious of what they were doing. They were not. To judge from the press, the attitude of backbenchers, and by-elections—and we have little other guide—English people were almost unanimous in wanting to win the war, and they wanted it run better, though they did not know how. Lloyd George had an answer: he could win the war. He had shown that he could produce munitions. He alone could manage Labour. Now he claimed the supreme direction. He proposed a war council of three, with himself in the chair, which should run the war free from control by the cabinet. His original target was Robertson, under whom he groaned at the war office. His target changed as the crisis developed. He came to demand that Asquith should be put on the shelf, more or less politely. By a curious twist, this demand was favoured even by Robertson, who did not yet appreciate the troubles in store for him from Lloyd George. Here was a dramatic conflict. On the one side, Lloyd George, man of the people, supported by almost the entire nation; on the other, Asquith, supported by every Cabinet minister, and mighty, as he believed, in the force of the two party machines.

Lloyd George could not launch the rebellion. It had to come from outside. Many backbench Unionists had long been restless against Asquith's Liberal negations. They were marshalled by Carson, always happiest in rebellion. On 8 November Carson almost captured a majority of the Unionists from Law over an apparently trivial question. Law took alarm. He was determined to maintain his leadership of the Unionist Party and appreciated now that he could do this only if he produced a more energetic conduct of the war. His adviser, Max Aitken, drew him steadily towards Lloyd George, and events drew him still more strongly. Law, like Lloyd George, did not spring from the charmed circle of traditional politics; in the last resort he, too, went with the people. Still, it seemed a terrifying prospect: two men of humble origin challenging the massed ranks of the established order.

But Asquith had feet of clay. His supremacy rested on the artificial silence

From A. J. P. Taylor, *English History 1914–1945* (London, 1965). Reprinted by permission of the Clarendon Press, Oxford, pp. 66–70, 104–105.

which the whips imposed on the house of commons. Now, not only the back-bench Unionists were turning against him. The Irish Nationalists had no interest in Asquith, and little in British politics, since the failure over Home Rule. Labour, though it supported Asquith, would equally support any other prime minister who could win the war. Above all, Christopher Addison, Lloyd George's only intimate who was in the house of commons, brought the sensational news that forty-nine Liberal members of parliament supported Lloyd George unconditionally and that another eighty would support him if he formed a government. This division in the Liberal party had been long a-growing. The Liberal leaders associated with Asquith, were men of excessive refinement—almost too fastidious for politics in peacetime, let alone at the turning point of a great war. Lloyd George's supporters were rougher in origin and in temperament: mostly Radical nonconformists, and self-made men in wool or engineering who were doing well out of the war. None was a banker, merchant, or financial magnate; none, a Londoner. Theirs was a long-delayed revolt of the provinces against London's political and cultural dominance: a revolt on behalf of the factories and workshops where the war was being won.

On December 1 Lloyd George formally proposed to Asquith a war council of three with himself in the chair. Asquith insisted that he himself must preside over the council and that it must be subordinated to the cabinet. Lloyd George wrote to Law: "The life of the country depends on resolute action by you now." On December 3 Law met his principal Unionist colleagues, led by the "three C's"—Robert Cecil, Austen Chamberlain, and Curzon. He told them that he intended to support Lloyd George. The Unionist leaders were angry at the little trouble-maker. They determined to resign, not in order to support Lloyd George, but rather to force an end to the conflict one way or the other. The same afternoon Law

gave the Unionists' decision to Asquith. Perhaps he did not make its meaning clear. Perhaps Asquith failed to grasp it. More probably Asquith was alarmed at the prospect of wholesale resignations. At any rate, he took the easy way out. He wrote to Lloyd George, accepting the war council as Lloyd George had proposed it. The crisis seemed over. To clinch things, Edwin Montagu, a Liberal who straddled between Asquith and Lloyd George, persuaded Asquith to inform the press that the government was about to be reconstructed. This was an announcement that Lloyd George had won and that Asquith would become a figurehead.

On December 4 the Liberal ministers, who had hitherto been kept in the dark, came to Asquith in high indignation. They demanded a fight. The "three C's" also indicated that they were on Asquith's side. Curzon declared that no Unionist except Law would join a Lloyd George government. As to himself, "I would rather die than serve under Lloyd George". Asquith repented of his weakness the evening before. He withdrew his agreement to Lloyd George's war council. On December 5 Lloyd George resigned. Asquith answered by resigning himself, thus bringing his government to an end. He defied Law or Lloyd George to form a government: "then they will have to come in on my terms." Asquith was not manœuvred out of office. He deliberately resigned office as a manœuvre to rout his critics. His complaints, when this manœuvre failed, were those of an aging heavyweight, who had been knocked out by a younger, more agile opponent.

The king, in accordance with constitutional practice, sent for Law, leader of the second great party. Law would form a government only if Asquith joined. Asquith refused. Even a conference at Buckingham Palace, proposed by Arthur Henderson and summoned by the king, did not move him. Law, Lloyd George, Balfour—he would serve under none of them. "What is the proposal? That I who have held first place for eight years should be asked to take a subordinate position." Law returned his commission and advised the king to send for Lloyd George. The king did so. The next morning, December 7, Lloyd George met the Labour M.P.'s and the national executive of the Labour party. He said to them:

Politicians make one fundamental mistake when they have been in office. They think that the people who are in office, or who have been in office, are absolutely essential to the Government of the country, and that no one else is in the least able to carry on affairs. Well, we are a nation of 45 millions, and, really, if we cannot produce at least two or three alternative Cabinets, we must really be what Carlyle once called us—"a nation of fools."

Thus Lloyd George appealed from the ruling classes to "the people." Labour, speaking for "the people," answered his call. In wartime the people mattered; and Lloyd George was home, once Labour backed him. Law delivered the backbench Unionists; Addison had gathered the backbench Liberals. Yet this government of the people was not composed of backbenchers after all. The Unionist leaders heard their country's call, or the call of office, once they saw that Lloyd George had succeeded. Balfour joined first, won by a promise of the foreign office. He declared: "you put a pistol at my head." The "three C's," including Curzon, yielded later in the day, on condition that neither Churchill nor Northcliffe was given office and that Haig remained commander-in-chief. On the other hand, all the prominent Liberals followed Asquith's lead, and stayed out. Asquith in fact, not Lloyd George, pursued a personal vendetta. He split the Liberal party and riveted on his adherents, however unwillingly, the appearance of opposing a government that was fighting the war. On the evening of December 7 Lloyd George returned to Buckingham Palace, and kissed hands as prime minister. He was the first son of the people to reach supreme power, or, as he put it himself, the first except Disraeli "who had not passed through the Staff College of the old Universities."

* * *

Lloyd George faced . . . immediate dangers at home. Under cover of the crisis in France, he got rid of Derby in April and sent Milner to the war office—civilian control asserted there at last. Milner's first act was to dismiss Robertson's satellite, Sir Frederick Maurice, the director of military operations. Maurice sought revenge. Disregarding the rule against public criticism of official superiors, he wrote to *The Times* on May 7 and accused Lloyd George of lying to the house of commons about the strength of the British army in France at the beginning of 1918. This was really a dead issue. There was no sense in quarrelling over the past, but in these uneasy days nerves were on edge, and few men judged sanely. The Squiffites thought that their chance had come. They pushed Asquith into demanding a select committee to inquire into the truth of Maurice's allegations. Lloyd George and Law at first lost courage. They offered an inquiry by two judges. Asquith refused the offer. Lloyd George had to face battle. He had the great asset that the attack came from Asquith. Carson, himself a virulent critic, attended a meeting of Unionist backbenchers, and reported sadly: "their hate of Asquith overrides all other considerations, and they will not back him tomorrow."

Lloyd George developed an unexpectedly good case. With miraculous sleight of hand, he showed that the figures of manpower which Maurice impugned, had been supplied from the war office by Maurice himself. Asquith, supinely obstinate to the last, did not withdraw his motion. Ninety-eight Liberals voted for it, and no Unionists—even Carson voted with the government. The attack had been bungled, as were most things which Asquith, or for that matter Maurice, had a hand in. The conspirators, if such they were, forgot the advice of F. E. Smith: "The man who enters into real and fierce controversy with Mr. Lloyd George must think clearly, think deeply, and think ahead. Otherwise he will think too late." The "Maurice debate," though irrelevant to the war, was of historic importance. The official Opposition had divided the house against the government for the only time in the war. The Liberal party was split in two, a split which was never healed. On May 9, 1918 the historic Liberal party committed suicide.

SUGGESTIONS FOR ADDITIONAL READING

This bibliography is highly selective, only indicating a few valuable studies on a topic which covers half a century, and touches on all aspects of English society. A few standard histories will provide an introduction. R. C. K. Ensor's *England, 1870-1914* (Oxford, 1936) is the most useful, a judicious mixture of information and judgements. A. J. P. Taylor's *English History, 1914-1945* (Oxford, 1965), in the same series is sound for the war years. Both volumes contain admirable bibliographies. Two older volumes which are still indispensable are Élie Halévy's *Epilogue* to his *A History of the English People in the Nineteenth Century. Epilogue I, 1895-1905* (London, 1926) and *Epilogue II, 1905-1914* (London, 1932) gave a brilliant analysis of the forces involved in the growth of collectivism. Less balanced, but valuable for its treatment of economic issues, is Keith Hutchison's *The Decline and Fall of British Capitalism* (New York, 1950). The obvious bias does not impair the usefulness of this study. More restricted in time, but wider in coverage, is *Edwardian England, 1901-1914* (London, 1964), a collection of essays edited by Simon Nowell-Smith. "The Political Scene" by Asa Briggs is especially helpful.

A narrative treatment of politics for the entire period is available in Ivor-Bulmer Thomas, *The Growth of the British Party System* (London, 1965, Vol. I). Also chronological and narrative is D. C. Somervell's *British Politics Since 1900* (New York, 1950). More substantial and analytical is *Party Politics* (Cambridge, 1961, Vol. II) by Ivor Jennings. A full-scale history of the Liberal party is such a formidable undertaking that it has yet to be written. There are two reliable summaries: Hamilton Fyfe, *The British Liberal Party: An Historical Sketch* (London, 1928), and Henry Slesser,

A History of the Liberal Party (London, 1944). W. Lyon Blease, *A Short History of English Liberalism* (London, 1913) is still useful. A more recent volume with a good introduction is *The Liberal Tradition: from Fox to Keynes* (London, 1956), edited by Alan Bullock and Maurice Shock.

For the most part, however, the student of the Liberal party must depend upon specialized studies. Good on the early composition of the party is John Vincent's *The Formation of the Liberal Party, 1857-1868* (London, 1966). Of interest is Donald Southgate's *The Passing of the Whigs, 1832-1886* (London, 1962), which explains "how, and when, and why the Whig party 'became' or 'developed into' or 'gave way to' the Liberal party." Party machinery and management receive close study by H. J. Hanham: *Elections and Party Management: Politics in the Time of Disraeli and Gladstone* (London, 1959). Interest groups and their effect on public policy are ably described by Samuel H. Beer in *British Politics* (London, 1965). An excellent study of party rivalries in the 1890's is provided by Peter Stansky: *Ambitions and Strategies: The Struggle for the Leadership of the Liberal Party in the 1890's* (New York, 1964). A thorough examination of the social legislation passed by the Liberals before the war is found in Bentley B. Gilbert's *The Evolution of National Insurance in Great Britain: The Origins of the Welfare State* (London, 1966). Gilbert also speculates on the collapse of the party. He claims that the Liberals took up social legislation too late and too hesitantly to save themselves.

A good essay on the development of political parties in the nineteenth century is provided by G. Kitson Clark in an introduction to R. T. Shannon's *Gladstone and the Bulgarian Agitation, 1876* (London,

1963). A series of Kitson Clark's lectures, printed as *The Making of Victorian England: Being the Ford Lectures Delivered Before the University of Oxford* (Cambridge, Massachusetts, 1962), also contain brilliant observations on society and political parties. The student should also read two excellent essays on Liberalism in the late nineteenth century: L. T. Hobhouse, *Liberalism* (London, 1911), and David Harris, "European Liberalism in the Nineteenth Century," *American Historical Review*, LX (April, 1955), pp. 501-526.

Radical aspirations in politics are deftly summarized in S. Maccoby's *The English Radical Tradition, 1763-1914* (London, 1952). A more extensive consideration of the same theme, chiefly through source materials, is available in his *English Radicalism* (London, 1938 and 1953, Vols. IV and V). A balanced examination of the two leading radicals in the Liberal party— Joseph Chamberlain and Lloyd George—is found in John W. Derby's *The Radical Tradition: Tom Paine to Lloyd George* (New York, 1967). Chamberlain's program for the 1880's is handled in his official life, *The Life of Joseph Chamberlain* (London, 1933, Vol. II) by J. L. Garvin. For this purpose the collected speeches, *Mr. Chamberlain's Speeches* (London, 1914, Vol. I) edited by Charles W. Boyd, are invaluable. An interesting thesis on Chamberlain's failure to capture the Liberal party in the 1880's is developed by R. T. Shannon in his *Gladstone and the Bulgarian Agitation, 1876*. Gladstone's return to politics on the Bulgarian issue, says Shannon, gave him a moral ascendency over the party which Chamberlain was unable to challenge. Gladstone and his moral campaigns thus diverted the party from its real interests and were "the ruin of Radicalism." Several biographies treat Lloyd George adequately. The fullest is Frank Owen's *Tempestuous Journey* (London, 1954), and the most perceptive is Thomas Jones, *Lloyd George* (London, 1951). Donald McCormick has written a capable but harshly critical volume, *The Mask of Merlin* (London, 1963). Frequent comments in E. L. Woodward's autobiographical *Short Journey* (London, 1942) suggest the keen distrust with which many Liberals viewed Lloyd George. His "sly, malignant oratory" and his few years of control over the party in the 1920's were "catastrophic," says Woodward, and prevented the creation of "a new liberal party."

The "New Liberalism" was ably defended by a number of young Liberals before the war. Herbert L. Samuel, drawing on the political theories of T. H. Green, outlined the principles of "contemporary Liberalism" in his *Liberalism* (London, 1902), to which Asquith provided an introduction. J. A. Hobson stressed the moral defects of *laissez-faire* competition in several volumes, especially *The Crisis of Liberalism: New Issues of Democracy* (London, 1909), and *The Industrial System: An Inquiry into Earned and Unearned Income* (London, 1909). Winston Churchill espoused much of Hobson's program in *Liberalism and the Social Problem* (London, 1909), a collection of his speeches between 1906 and 1909. The philosophical justification for this trend towards collectivism in public affairs was given by T. H. Green in his "Lectures on the Principles of Political Obligation," found in *Works of Thomas Hill Green* (London, 1894-1900, volume two), edited by Richard L. Nettleship. A clear summary and good analysis of his political theories are given in Melvin Richter's *The Politics of Conscience, T. H. Green and his Age* (London, 1964, Chapters 8-10).

Few studies exist on Nonconformity and the Liberals. A good introduction is provided by John F. Glaser, "English Nonconformity and the Decline of Liberalism," *American Historical Review*, LXIII (January, 1958), pp. 352-363. On Home Rule and the party, the single most important study is J. L. Hammond's *Gladstone and the Irish Nation* (London, 1938). The account is sympathetic but not uncritical. Chamberlain's position is developed by J. L. Garvin in the official life, while accounts favorable to Gladstone are contributed by John Morley, *The Life of William Ewert Gladstone* (London, 1903, Vol. III), and Geoffry T. Garratt, *The Two Mr. Gladstones* (London, 1936).

Several general volumes are helpful in a consideration of Labour-Liberal relations: Frank Bealey and Henry Pelling, *Labour and Politics, 1900-1906: A History of the Labour Representation Committee* (New York, 1958); Philip Poirier, *The Advent of the Labour Party* (New York, 1958) and Henry Pelling's *Origins of the Labour Party* (London, 1954). Paul Richard Thompson, *Socialists, Liberals and Labour: the Struggle for London, 1885-1914* (London, 1967) has made a good case study of the Liberal failure to capture the Labour vote in a great metropolitan center. His thesis is summarized in an article, "Liberals, Radicals and Labour in London 1880-1890," appearing in *Past and Present*, XXVII (April, 1964), pp. 73-101.

The effects of the First World War on the party are closely analyzed by Trevor Wilson in *The Downfall of the Liberal Party, 1914-1935* (London, 1966). Few competent studies are available on wartime politics. Exceptions are A. J. P. Taylor's *Politics and Warfare and Other Essays* (London, 1965), and Lord Beaverbrook's *Politicians and the War, 1914-1916* (London, 1928 and 1932, two volumes). Both studies are critical of the Asquith Liberals and sympathetic to Lloyd George. The side of Asquith is upheld in an official

biography: A. J. Spender and Cyril Asquith, *The Life of Lord Oxford and Asquith* (London, 1932). Roy Jenkins gives a balanced treatment of the contending parties in *Asquith* (London, 1965). The fullest and most rigorously historical account of the 1918 election is Trevor Wilson's "The Coupon and the British General Election of 1918," *The Journal of Modern History*, XXXVI (March, 1964), pp. 28-42.

Any study of the Liberal party must also include biographies of the leading party figures. In addition to those already mentioned, the student will wish to consult some of the following: John A. Spender, *Life of Sir Henry Campbell-Bannerman* (London, 1923, two volumes); Violet Bonham Carter, *Winston Churchill: An Intimate Portrait* (New York, 1965); Bernard H. Holland, *The Life of Spencer Compton, Eighth Duke of Devonshire* (London, 1911, two volumes) and Lord Edmond Fitzmaurice, *The Life of Granville* (London, 1903, two volumes). George M. Trevelyan has contributed a good biography of *Grey of Fallodon* (London, 1937), and Roy Jenkins has a study of *Sir Charles Dilke, A Victorian Tragedy* (London, 1958), which explains why Dilke was unable to reach his full promise. Others are: Alfred George Gardiner, *The Life of Sir William Harcourt* (London, 1923, two volumes), and an excellent recent study, *Rosebery* (London, 1963) by Robert Rhodes James.